The
FITNESS
HANDBOOK

The FITNESS HANDBOOK

Planning your personal fitness programme and keeping to it

ANN GOODSELL
FOREWORD BY
SALLY GUNNELL

MARSHALL PUBLISHING • LONDON

A Marshall Edition
Conceived, edited and designed by
Marshall Editions Ltd
The Orangery
161 New Bond Street
London W1Y 9PA

First published in the UK in 1994 by
Boxtree Ltd
This edition published in 1999 by
Marshall Publishing Ltd

ISBN 1 84028 107 3

Editor	Anne Yelland
Designer	Simon Adamczewski
DTP Editor	Mary Pickles
DTP Designer	Jonathan Bigg
Photographer	Matthew Ward
Editorial Director	Ruth Binney
Managing Editor	Lindsay McTeague
Production	Janice Storr
	Nikki Ingram
	Kate Waghorn

Originated in the UK by Kestrel
Lithographic Reproductions Ltd,
Chelmsford
Printed and bound in Italy by New
Interlitho SpA, Milan

CONTENTS

Foreword by Sally Gunnell MBE 7

Why a personal trainer? 8

Part One: Assessing Your Fitness 10–39
*How your body works, testing your fitness and starting
an exercise programme.*

Part Two: Your Personal Fitness Programme 40–197

Menus 40
*From beginners' to expert, for men
and women.*

Endurance Programmes 56
*Improving your aerobic fitness through walking,
jogging, swimming, rowing, cycling and skipping.*

Exercises for Strength 74
*Building strength in your legs, shoulders, back, chest,
arms and abdominals.*

Exercises for Flexibility 150
*Improving the mobility of your neck, shoulders, arms,
back, chest, buttocks, hips, thighs, calves and
abdominals.*

Extending your Programme 184
*Circuit training, cross training, speciality menus,
advice on gyms and coping with injuries.*

Part Three: Eating for Health 204–215
What to eat and drink to stay fit and healthy.

Scorecards 216

Index & Acknowledgments 220

FOREWORD

I first met Ann Goodsell when I went along to a local aerobics class. Ann was the teacher. I didn't keep up the aerobics (the classes were too busy) but I did remember Ann's enthusiasm and vitality and her concern that everyone enjoyed and gained something from the classes.

In 1990, when I was looking for someone to work with me to ensure that my body was in the best possible condition and shape, I contacted Ann. By then, she was concentrating on teaching privately. She took me on and injected the same energy she had put into those aerobics classes into her sessions with me.

Week by week, she set me targets, monitored my progress, and corrected my exercise technique until she was happy that I was as strong and flexible as I could be. Without the work Ann did with me to complement that of my running and hurdling coach, Bruce Longden, I would not have had the calm confidence in my ability to win that overtook me on the Barcelona track and gave me my Olympic gold medal.

Ann's book follows the same pattern she uses with all her clients: continual assessment, individual programmes to suit individual goals, clear and concise instructions and practical tips, all infused with her infectious enthusiasm for her subject.

Like me, you will benefit from Ann's personal approach no matter who you are when you begin and where you want to go. Once you're on your way, she will keep you going as she has kept me on the right track. You will find that the pursuit of fitness becomes addictive – and there's a whole new set of goals after you've won Olympic gold.

Sally Gunnell

Sally Gunnell MBE

400m hurdles
1993   World Record Holder and
        World Champion
1992   Olympic Gold Medallist
1990   Commonwealth Gold
        Medallist and Record Holder

100m hurdles
1988   British Record Holder

WHY A PERSONAL TRAINER?

I have been concerned with fitness and fitness teaching for many years, working with groups and on a one-to-one basis. What I have learned is that most people can do most things if they are sufficiently motivated and if their goals are realistic to begin with.

When I take on a new client, we discuss at length what they want to achieve, and the reasons they have decided that now is the time to start working toward that. For most people, there has to be a catalyst: new boyfriend/girlfriend, impending marriage, invitation to join a Sunday team, corporate membership of a gym, holiday of a lifetime, "big" birthday (usually either 30 or 40).

Their goals are as diverse as their reasons for starting a fitness programme: wanting to run a marathon, swim a mile, try a cycling holiday, look good on the beach, or simply feel good. Sometimes they are recovering from an injury and need to build their strength. All of these are goals that I can help people work toward. People I cannot really help are those who say "I want to look like Arnold Schwarzenegger" or "I want to look like Cindy Crawford". That is impossible: those people are born with the capacity to achieve those looks and the vast majority of the rest of us are not.

First of all, I always suggest that someone takes a good hard look in the mirror. I also test their basic fitness, their strength, aerobic endurance and flexibility. Once we have done that, we both know that we are working toward the same realistic goals. Before you read any further make a list of your short- and long-term goals (next week, next month, in six months, next year). Do they appear to be realistic?

I don't promise an easy time and I don't promise fast results. I say to most people that they will notice a good improvement in six months and an even better one in a year if they keep at it. They still may not run their marathon or lift 20 kilos or have the muscle definition they desire, but they will be well on the way with a safe and effective programme.

We work out a programme together. I take note of their likes and dislikes and if there is some activity that a client knows they will not be able to keep up, I don't include it. We usually meet two or three times a week so that I can monitor progress, check technique, encourage and, above all, motivate.

Depending on their goals and their progress, every month or three months, I test again so that we can both see what effect the programme is having. Sometimes we modify an activity or exercise, or add an extra session. Eventually, hopefully, my clients are where they want to be: feeling mentally and physically good, with changed eating habits, a heart that works well, muscles they can be proud of and a level of flexibility they thought they had left behind when they quit their teens.

It isn't easy but then nothing worthwhile ever is. I was sporty at school and even considered a career as a physical training instructor before I decided to spend my late teens and early twenties having what I considered then to be a good time: late nights, parties, drinking and smoking. I got myself in good shape, then let it slide three or four times before I finally realized that being fit meant changing my habits to party occasionally instead of every night. In doing so, I increased my chances of living longer – and learned that natural "highs" can beat induced ones. It's my firm belief that fitness is always worth the sacrifices on your time and can be great fun.

This book is structured along the lines I use when I work one to one. In effect, I am working on a one-to-one basis with you. For me, that is the ideal way to approach a fitness programme: I wish I had had a personal trainer years ago. Some classes are excellent but (believe me) class teachers can't watch everyone *and* offer constructive advice to all those who need it, even with the most limited of numbers and the most gifted and committed teacher.

I cannot watch you do the exercises but if you read them carefully before you try to do them and have a dummy run for those you are unsure of to get the correct technique before you start lifting weights, you will be getting the same help as if I were there.

The tips that accompany many of the exercises are those I have learned to be of most use in my years of teaching. I say most of them at least once a day to reinforce correct technique.

I love what I do: there are few things more satisfying than helping people achieve their goals and unlock the true self that they (and I) know is inside. And it isn't a one-way process. Everyone I have ever worked with has given me something in return. A lot of what I have learned from them has gone into this book.

The only people I turn down are those whose goals are unrealistic and those who I sense are not serious about their fitness. With those provisos, whatever you want to achieve, I hope you will find what you need to get there in this book.

A. Goodsell

Ann Goodsell

WHAT IS FITNESS?

It is easy to say "I want to be fitter": most of us say it often. Defining fitness, however, is more problematic. For a start, there are many different kinds of fitness. A marathon runner could not go five sets any more easily than a tennis champion could run a marathon. Yet both are supremely fit.

Fitness also means different things to different people. Some of us do want to be fitter to play a sport, or we have a fixed ambition (to run a marathon, or cycle round Europe). Many of us, however, simply want to feel better, to look good, have some energy left at the end of the day, be emotionally stable and have some fun. We don't enjoy being overweight, tired and under constant stress – the staple elements of life in the 1990s.

Fitness training can help you on all these levels. It will make you a better sports player, if that is what you want, but it will also cut down your body fat in favour of muscle (so you may lose weight) and tone these new muscles, thereby improving your appearance. It will give you strength and stamina, help you relax and improve your ability to sleep. Taking regular exercise increases your speed of movement and helps your coordination and concentration. Finally, it promotes the feeling of wellbeing that only comes from doing something by yourself for yourself.

This book is primarily concerned with overall fitness, of which there are three components: aerobic endurance; strength (often divided into muscular strength and muscular endurance); and flexibility. We all tend to be good at one or two of these (with flexibility the most neglected area), but your aim should be to reach a good standard in all three, and in every part of your body.

Aerobic exercise is vital: a strong, healthy heart and efficient lungs are the foundations of a fit and healthy lifestyle. In later life, will you be able to play with your grandchildren, or run to catch the train? Heart attacks do not always happen to others and although many people recover from them, their lives are never the same again.

Working toward strong muscles does not mean that you have to be muscle bound. Muscular strength and muscular endurance mean good support for your skeleton and improved posture. These factors alone will stand you in good stead as you get older. Healthy, strong muscles also give your body shape and tone.

Flexibility will keep you mobile as you age. It is a sobering thought that many mobility problems suffered by elderly people could have been avoided.

You may well have discovered the reasons why this multiple approach is so important without being aware of them. Women, in particular, attend aerobics classes and fail to see a difference in their body shape. This is because there is not enough all-round fitness development in aerobic dance classes. To change your shape a programme that combines aerobic and strength training is necessary.

Men, on the other hand, play a weekend soccer or rugby game and in time are plagued by knee and hamstring problems, largely because they do no flexibility work. Stamina and strength are only part of the overall picture: you must also stretch.

If your goal is to improve your fitness level, read the introductory section, test yourself (pp. 22–27), then look at the overall assessment to see what to do next.

OTHER TYPES OF FITNESS
This book can also be used by those who do not primarily want an improvement in overall fitness. First read the introduction and test yourself: if you want to train for a sport, turn to pp. 192–97; if your goal is aerobic fitness above all, choose a programme from pp. 58–73; if you want to strength train or body tone, work from the strength exercises on pp. 78–149.

Finally, a word of warning. Whatever your major aim, don't neglect the other components of fitness: a whole-body approach is important. The aerobics programmes include complementary strength exercises: use them. And, as you strengthen a part of your body, stretch it too.

An exercise bicycle offers an effective way of improving your aerobic fitness, one of the keys to a healthy and longer life.

YOUR BODY AND EXERCISE

The most basic measure of your fitness is the way your heart performs. The heart is a muscular organ whose contractions pump blood around the body and deliver the oxygen it contains (which enters the body through the lungs) to your muscles. Like all other muscles, the heart needs a constant supply of oxygen to function. Unlike other muscles, however, the heart has to work all the time to sustain life.

Since it is a muscle, you can train your heart to improve its performance. The way to do this is to increase the amount of work your muscles are doing, by starting to jog, for example. To meet the increased demand for oxygen from the muscles, your heart has to pump more blood around your body, so improving the efficiency of your heart also has an effect on your lungs, circulatory and respiratory systems. This type of training is known as aerobic (meaning using oxygen).

Over time, as you train your aerobic system, your body becomes more efficient at taking oxygen from the blood. As this happens your heart starts to beat more slowly and strongly; it has to do less work to achieve the same results.

Many people who decide that they wish to be fitter do so because of the obvious benefits to their heart, lungs and circulation. The other major benefit of aerobic work, however, is that it boosts your metabolic rate, that is the rate at

The initial stages of an activity use the body's energy reserves which are soon depleted. Increased demand triggers the aerobic system.

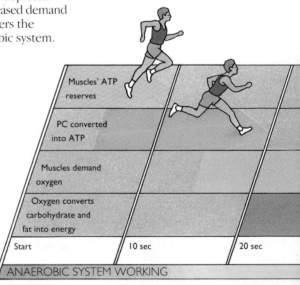

ANAEROBIC
Reserves of ATP stored in the muscles allow you to work for about 10 seconds. Then, more is synthesized through the action of PC (phosphate creatine) to give another 10 seconds. Energy after this comes from glycogen, the waste product of which is lactic acid.

Muscles' ATP reserves

PC converted into ATP

Muscles demand oxygen

Oxygen converts carbohydrate and fat into energy

Start   10 sec   20 sec

ANAEROBIC SYSTEM WORKING

which you burn food for energy. If you follow an aerobic training programme and eat sensibly, you should also lose body fat.

Not all activities depend on the efficiency of your body's aerobic system. The muscles themselves contain reserves of energy which can be called upon for short bursts of activity (running to catch the bus or train) or for some sporting activities – sprinting, for example.

Your muscles work in this way for between 10 and 30 seconds before fatigue sets in: your muscles start to become heavy (this is due to the build up of lactic acid). This type of activity is known as anaerobic (meaning without oxygen). All exercise of high intensity and brief duration uses the body's anaerobic system.

Depending on what you are looking for from a fitness programme, you can choose to train your aerobic or anaerobic system, or both. If you want to run a marathon, concentrate on aerobic work. As your heart and lungs start to work more efficiently you will be able to run for longer distances before you become tired. Other aerobic activities include stepping, dancing, roller and ice skating, cross-country skiing and the suggestions on pp. 58–73.

If your aim is to sprint or hurdle well, play tennis or squash or power lift (the major anaerobic activities), concentrate on boosting your ATP (adenosine triphosphate) reserves and your tolerance to the build up of lactic acid by short sharp bursts of activity. In this way you increase the time before your aerobic system comes into play.

If you want to improve both systems, put together a cross-training programme of activities of both types (see pp. 190–91).

10 min

AEROBIC SYSTEM WORKING

AEROBIC
Your aerobic system starts to work as ATP reserves are used up. Stored carbohydrate and fat are converted into energy. For 1–2 minutes both systems work together; then the aerobic system takes over. After 10 minutes, 85% of your energy derives from your aerobic system.

YOUR BODY • Bones and joints

The three most important functions of the skeleton are to support and shape the body; to protect its vulnerable internal organs; and to provide the framework to which muscles are attached.

Bones themselves are too rigid to bend, but the more than 200 bones of the body are held together at joints by flexible connective tissue. All movements that change the position of the bony parts of the body occur at joints. The structure of a joint and the nature of the connective tissue determine how freely it moves. The tighter the bones fit together, the stronger the joint but the more restricted the movement around that joint.

Joints at which there is no cavity (or space) between the bones, and where the tissue between the bones is fibrous, are classed as immovable. Joints at which there is no cavity but the bones are joined by cartilage allow restricted movement. Those at which there is a cavity, known as the synovial cavity, allow free movement. As such, these are the joints that are most likely to sustain an injury.

At synovial joints, the bones are not joined by cartilage, although the ends of the bones are covered by cartilage which acts as a shock absorber, nor by fibrous tissue; instead there is no break in the fibrous tissue that surrounds the bones. The walls of a synovial cavity are lined by synovial membrane which secretes fluid to lubricate the joint. Many muscles are attached at synovial joints and when you warm up (see pp. 36–37) you get this secretion process underway.

Synovial joints are held together by ligaments, bands of fibrous tissue. The degree of movement around a synovial joint is determined by the type of joint (there are six) and by the position of the ligaments, tendons and muscles attached to the bones.

Ball and socket joints allow free movement in all directions. Many muscles are attached at ball and socket joints which makes warming up vital. Hinge joints allow movement in one plane only; gliding joints are usually flat and allow side-to-side and back-and-forth movements; at pivot joints, movement is rotational. Condyloid and saddle joints allow flexion and extension only.

AVOIDING PROBLEMS

One way to avoid problems with your bones is to ensure that the muscles that support them are strong and flexible. Good posture is also important (see p. 77). Finally, be sure to warm up thoroughly.

SYNOVIAL JOINTS
A Neck: pivot
B Shoulder: ball and socket; where humerus fits into clavicle: condyloid
C Elbow: hinge
D Wrist: pivot; base of the thumb: saddle
E Fingers: gliding
F Hip: ball and socket
G Knee: hinge
H Ankle: hinge

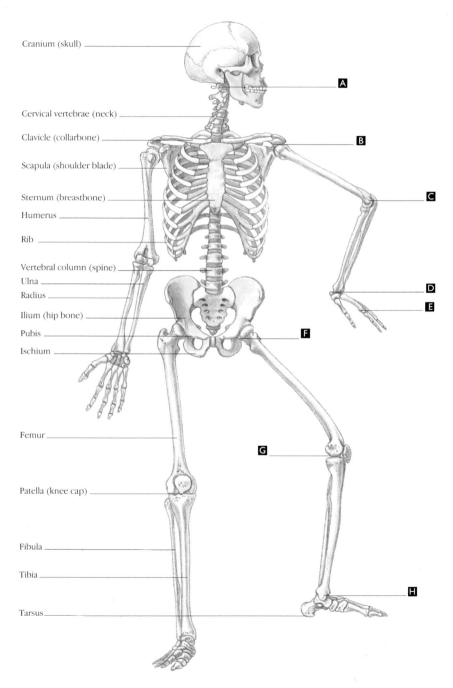

Cranium (skull)

A

Cervical vertebrae (neck)

Clavicle (collarbone)

B

Scapula (shoulder blade)

Sternum (breastbone)

C

Humerus

Rib

Vertebral column (spine)

Ulna

D

Radius

E

Ilium (hip bone)

Pubis

F

Ischium

Femur

G

Patella (knee cap)

Fibula

Tibia

Tarsus

H

YOUR BODY • Muscles and tendons

The body contains some 650 voluntary muscles (muscles over which you have control). Voluntary muscles are attached to the skeleton and enable you to move and to keep upright. The type of fibres that comprise your muscles (see pp. 18–19), the length of the muscle belly (or core) and the strength of the muscles are the factors that limit what your body can achieve.

Tendons are similar to, but composed of stronger tissue than, muscles. A muscle may tear, a tendon is less likely to. Tendons form the attachment between muscle and bone. The strongest tendon, the Achilles, joins the gastrocnemius and ankle.

You do not need to understand what each muscle does to follow a fitness programme. But it is important to know the major muscle groups (since these are the ones you will be using) and what happens when you make demands on them. Each strength and flexibility exercise in the book indicates which muscle(s) that exercise works: "feeling" the exercise in the right place is one of the surest ways to tell that you are doing it correctly.

It is also important to remember to work opposing muscle groups so that your body is balanced. For

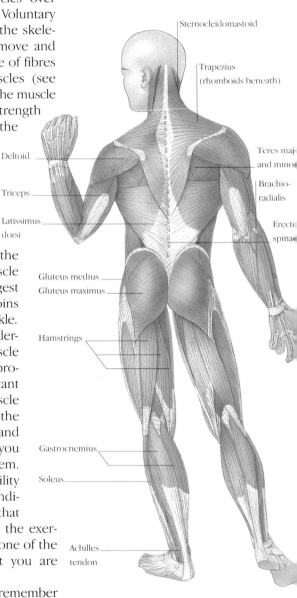

Sternocleidomastoid

Trapezius
(rhomboids beneath)

Teres major
and minor

Brachio-
radialis

Erector
spinae

Deltoid

Triceps

Latissimus
dorsi

Gluteus medius
Gluteus maximus

Hamstrings

Gastrocnemius

Soleus

Achilles
tendon

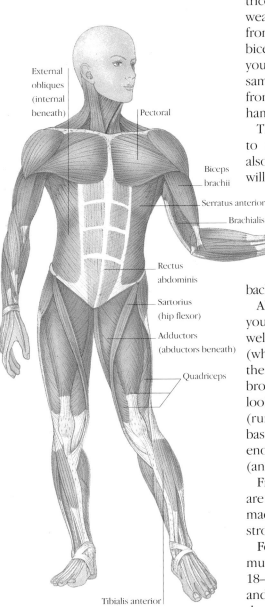

External obliques (internal beneath)

Pectoral

Biceps brachii

Serratus anterior

Brachialis

Rectus abdominis

Sartorius (hip flexor)

Adductors (abductors beneath)

Quadriceps

Tibialis anterior

example, in many people the triceps (at the back of the arm) are weak while the biceps (at the front) are strong; working your biceps without your triceps puts your triceps under stress. The same is true for quadriceps (at the front of the upper leg) and hamstrings (at the back).

This principle not only applies to opposing muscle groups but also to parts of the body (you will find that the phrase "whole-body approach" recurs repeatedly). Strong pectorals (at the front of your chest) will, if you neglect the upper back, contribute to round shoulders.

Also, consider what strengthening your muscles can do for you. A well-developed latissimus dorsi (which connects the backbone to the upper arm) can give you a broad-shouldered, narrow-waisted look; a strong erector spinae (running along the spine from its base to chest height) contributes enormously to an upright posture (and helps avert backache).

Finally, remember that muscles are tolerant of the demands being made on them but not infinitely strong or pliable: take care.

For further information on how muscles are composed see pp. 18–19 and fuelled see pp. 10–11 and 210–11; for details of how to develop and maintain muscle, see pp. 74–75 and 150–51.

YOUR BODY•Types and potential

Regardless of the goals of your fitness programme, your body may impose limitations on what you can achieve. Take a look in the mirror. What is your predominant body type (*below*)? There are three basic types and although "pure" examples of any are rare, most people lean toward one more than the others.

Your overall type determines your capacity for muscular development and also therefore the range of activities to which you are most suited. Generally, endomorphs tend toward cycling, walking, swimming and both low-impact and water aerobics; mesomorphs toward weight training, circuit training, martial arts, skiing and racket sports; and ectomorphs toward ballet, marathon running, cycling, aerobic dance and weight training.

Equally vital in determining your goals is the shape you are in. Here, height and weight charts are meaningless: the most reliable indicator of whether you need to lose weight is your percentage of body fat and where that fat is concentrated. This is governed by body type and gender: men carry

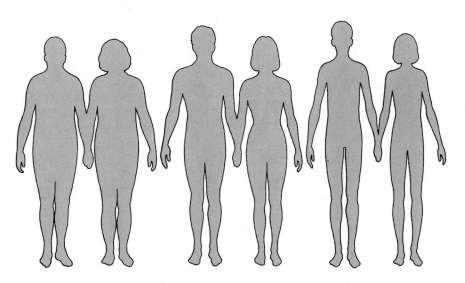

Endomorphs: small bones; large head; drooping shoulders; large chest/breasts; short neck and limbs; heavy buttocks; wide hips; gain weight easily.

Mesomorphs: heavy bones; broad chest and shoulders; classic triangular shape; good development potential; carry little excess body fat.

Ectomorphs: long bones; slim; long neck and limbs; short trunk; narrow chest and buttocks; little body fat; low potential for muscular growth.

fat at the waist, shoulders and upper arms; women at the waist, hips, thighs, upper arms, breasts and below the shoulder blades.

Fitness consultants use callipers to measure body fat accurately. To test yourself, hold your arm as shown below and grip as much flesh as you can from the back of your arm. If you can pinch 2.5cm (1in) or more, you should shed body fat; include plenty of aerobic work in your programme.

The third factor that has an effect on your fitness programme is the composition of your muscle fibres and their capacity for development (*below*). Muscle-belly lengths are usually consistent in the upper and lower body, so your calf and biceps are good indicators of the development potential of all your muscles. The longer the muscle, the greater its potential.

Most people's muscles are composed of equal percentages of slow-twitch fibres (for long periods of low-intensity work) and fast-twitch fibres (for short bursts of high-intensity work). A higher proportion of slow-twitch fibres, however, limits your muscular growth potential.

To test your calf, stand on one leg, supporting all your weight on your toes. Mark the end of the bulge of muscle near your heel. For your biceps, bend your arm and make a tight fist. Feel where the muscle begins near your elbow.

If your calf muscle bulges near your knee (*left*), you have little potential for growth. If you can get three fingers between your biceps and elbow, at its most fully developed, your biceps will resemble a tennis ball under the skin.

If your muscle stops midway down your calf, or you can fit two fingers between your biceps and elbow (*right*), you have medium growth potential. A muscle that almost reaches your heel, or a biceps that leaves room for one finger (*left*), has the greatest potential.

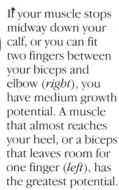

YOUR HEART RATE

To ensure that you are working at the correct level of intensity for your body, you need to be able to monitor your heart rate before, during and after exercise. The pulse offers the easiest identifiable measure of your heart rate and although taking a pulse can be tricky at first, with practice it will become part of your routine.

For best results determine your resting pulse rate first thing in the morning when you are relaxed and before the strains of the day start to have an effect. You will need a watch with a second hand.

As you do more aerobic work and the efficiency of your heart increases, your resting pulse rate should fall. Keep a record to check.

HOW TO TAKE YOUR PULSE

1 With the first two fingers of your right hand, draw an imaginary line from your right ear to the widest part of your jaw.

2 Lower your fingers under your jawline into the firm strip of muscle running down your neck.

3 You should now be able to feel the throb of your carotid artery beneath your fingertips.

4 Press gently.

5 When you have found the pulse, start by counting 0 for the first beat, then 1, 2, 3 and so on for 10 seconds.

6 Once you are confident that you are feeling and counting accurately, multiply your 10-second count by 6 to get your resting heart rate.

7 Repeat the test during exercise sessions to be sure that you are working within your TTZ and not above a safe maximum.

RESTING PULSE RATE				
MEN				
Age	Poor	Fair	Good	Excellent
20–29	86+	70–84	62–68	60 or less
30–39	86+	72–84	64–70	62 or less
40–49	90+	74–88	66–72	64 or less
50+	90+	76–88	68–74	66 or less
WOMEN				
20–29	96+	78–94	72–76	70 or less
30–39	98+	80–96	72–78	70 or less
40–49	100+	80–98	74–78	72 or less
50+	104+	84–102	76–82	74 or less

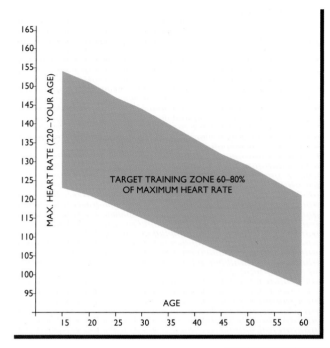

The graph (*left*) gives an at-a-glance indication of your target training zone (TTZ). Find your age along the horizontal axis, then read off the upper and lower limits of your training zone on the vertical axis. The core work of any training session should fall within these limits.

TARGET TRAINING ZONE (TTZ)

In theory, you could work at any intensity; in practice there are limits beyond which it is not safe to push your heart. Your maximum heart rate is judged to be 220 minus your age. There is a complex mathematical formula by which to determine your pulse rate during exercise, but it is simpler to use the graph (*above*).

During your warm up (see pp. 36–37), you should aim to raise your pulse from its resting rate to between 40% and 50% of its maximum. As the work of the session gets underway, push the rate to between 60% and 80%. Don't exceed the upper limit.

PERSONAL TRAINER'S TIPS

• Taking your pulse in your wrist can be tricky. Turn your right wrist under side up. Place the first two fingers of your left hand about 2.5cm (1in) from your wrist.
• The most accurate method of taking your pulse is to use a pulse monitor. Follow the directions provided with the apparatus.

TESTING YOUR ENDURANCE

Finding out how fit you are now is the first essential step in your detailed fitness analysis. The way to do this is to test your ability in the three basic areas: aerobic endurance, muscular strength and flexibility. The results of the tests on these pages will enable you to pinpoint where you should begin your fitness programme.

These tests are personal. You may find it useful to work with a partner in order to ensure accurate results, but the tests should not be used competitively. Everyone is different and, broadly speaking, one person's strength is another's weakness. Don't be disheartened if your results are not as good as someone else's or if you seem to have made less improvement than they have.

With all the tests, be sure to warm up thoroughly before you begin (see pp. 36–37). Keep a record of your results and include the time of day you did the test and a note on how you felt afterward. When you repeat a test, always do so at the same time of day for the most accurate results.

Your aerobic endurance is the efficiency with which your heart works (see also pp. 12–13 and 56–57). To test your aerobic fitness you need first to determine your resting pulse rate (see pp. 20–21). The test itself gives an indication of how effectively your heart and lungs feed oxygen to your muscles by determining the time it takes your heart to slow down after exercise. Don't attempt the test if your resting heart rate is in the poor category. See your doctor.

Your recovery rate is an essential part of your fitness assessment. Repeat the test at the end of each 10-week menu (pp. 40–55) or programme (pp. 58–73) and chart its improvement as you progress through the fitness levels.

RECOVERY PULSE RATE AFTER 30 SECONDS				
MEN				
Age	Poor	Fair	Good	Excellent
20–29	102+	86–100	76–84	74 or less
30–39	102+	88–100	80–86	78 or less
40–49	106+	90–104	82–88	80 or less
50+	106+	92–104	84–90	82 or less
WOMEN				
20–29	112+	94–110	88–92	86 or less
30–39	114+	96–112	88–94	86 or less
40–49	116+	96–114	90–94	88 or less
50+	118+	100–116	92–98	90 or less

THE STEP TEST

Breathe normally throughout.

PHASE 1

1 Stand no more than 30cm (12in) away from a step, stair or bench less than 20–25cm (8–10in) high.

2 Keep your back straight, chest lifted and abdominals in.

3 Bend your knees slightly and tuck your buttocks under your hips. Place both hands on your hips.

4 Take a step up: place your heel down first, then the ball of your foot. Don't lean forward and keep your torso erect as you step.

PHASE 2

5 Step up and down (right foot up, left up, right down and left down) as fast as you comfortably can for 3 minutes.

6 Sit down. Time 30 seconds, then take your pulse.

Results: If your recovery rate is poor or fair, start with a beginners' programme or menu; if your recovery is good or excellent, start at intermediate level and move up a level if you find it too easy.

SAFETY WARNING

A resting heart rate in the poor category is sufficient in itself to tell you that your aerobic fitness is poor. See your doctor. If you feel breathless, nauseous or dizzy during the test, stop immediately and consult your doctor.

23

TESTING YOUR STRENGTH

Strength is the ability of your muscles to complete and sustain a movement against a resistance. Strong muscles support your skeleton and help to keep your body upright. Once you reach a certain strength level, you may choose to work on your muscular endurance, toning and shaping your muscles without expecting them to grow further. In either case, you must first determine your current strength rating. See pp. 74–75 for more information on strength.

In order to test your muscular strength and interpret the results of the test effectively, you will have to make a preliminary judgement of your fitness, based on the definitions given below.

ASSESSING THE RESULTS

There is considerable overlap in the categories so take an average when you are deciding the level that is most appropriate for you and change to another level if you find things too easy or difficult. If you judged yourself a beginner or intermediate and two or more of your results are poor or fair, start with a beginners' menu. If two or more of your results are good or excellent, start at intermediate level (but move to beginners' if you find it difficult). If you judged yourself advanced or expert and two or more of your results were poor or fair, start with an intermediate menu; if two or more were good or excellent, start with an advanced menu.

BEGINNER	INTERMEDIATE	ADVANCED	EXPERT
You never take any exercise and/or you are more than 50	You have exercised intermittently in the past year	You exercise regularly, at least 3–4 times per week	You are a sports player or have a sporting lifestyle

PRESS UPS

1 Make an assessment of your level, then choose an appropriate press up position (see pp. 102–4).

2 Do as many reps as you can with good technique.

3 Keep a note of your result.

UPPER BODY STRENGTH					
Level		Poor	Fair	Good	Excellent
BEG.	Standing wall press	1–5	6–10	11–19	20+
INTER.	Box press up	1–5	6–10	11–19	20+
ADV.	¾ press	1–5	6–10	11–19	20+
EXP.	Full press up	1–5	6–10	11–19	20+

ABDOMINAL HOLD

Breathe normally throughout.

PHASE 1
1 Sit with your back straight and abdominals in. Bend your knees and place your feet flat on the floor, hip width apart.

PHASE 2
2 Slowly lean back. When your outstretched hands are above your knees, hold.

3 Keep your back flat and abs tight: hold as long as you comfortably can. Keep a note of your result.

MIDDLE BODY STRENGTH				
Level		Poor	Fair	Good	Excellent
BEG.	in seconds	0–9	10–19	20–29	30+
INTER.	in seconds	20–29	30–39	40–49	50+
ADV.	in seconds	40–49	50–59	60–79	80+
EXP.	in seconds	60–79	80–99	100–119	120+

WALL SITS

Breathe normally throughout.

1 Stand 60cm (2ft) away from a wall, with your feet hip width apart and your toes forward.

2 Bend at your knees and hips and press your lower back into the wall. Try to get a 90° angle at your hips and knees, as if you were sitting on a chair.

3 Keep your chest lifted, abdominals in and shoulders relaxed.

4 Hold as long as you comfortably can. Keep a note of your result.

LOWER BODY STRENGTH				
Level		Poor	Fair	Good	Excellent
BEG.	in seconds	20–29	30–39	40–49	50+
INTER.	in seconds	40–49	50–59	60–79	80+
ADV.	in seconds	60–79	80–99	100–119	120+
EXP.	in seconds	100–119	120–139	140–159	160+

TESTING YOUR FLEXIBILITY

Flexibility is your ability to take your muscles through their full range of movement around a joint or joints (see also pp. 150–51). Before you test your flexibility, warm up thoroughly (pp. 36–37). Use the same tests every time and test at the same time of day. Repeat each test three times, taking the best "score" as your result. It is easier to get accurate results if you have a partner to measure for you. The results give a broad indication of your overall flexibility.

SIT AND REACH
Areas worked: Back of thighs, hips
Muscles used: Hamstrings, hip flexors

PHASE ■
1 Sit with your legs extended and feet flexed.

2 Keep your back straight, chest lifted, head in line with your spine and abdominals in. Look forward.

3 Keeping your arms straight, breathe in as you reach skyward.

PHASE ■
4 Stretch up leading with your fingertips, then breathe out as you slowly and smoothly bend forward from your hips.

5 Keep your back flat as you reach for your toes.

6 Don't crane your neck in an attempt to reach further.

7 Measure the distance between your middle finger and your toes.

SIT AND REACH RESULTS	
ZONE	
1 — Finger more than 12.5cm (5in) from toes	Most people lack flexibility in this area but good hip flexion is important for many sports **ZONE 1** You definitely need to do more stretching
2 — Finger reaches, or almost reaches, toes	**ZONE 2** You are fairly flexible but should do more stretching
3 — Finger extends past toes 2.5cm (1in) or more	**ZONE 3** You have good flexibility: stretch to maintain it

SHOULDER EXTENSION **Areas worked:** Back of arms **Muscles used:** Triceps

Breathe normally throughout.

1 Stand with your back straight, abdominals in and pelvis forward. Bend your knees slightly.

2 Reach up with your right arm, bend at the elbow and drop your hand over your shoulder.

3 Bend your left arm at the elbow and reach up behind your back.

4 Slowly move your hands toward each other. Try to make your fingertips meet.

SHOULDER EXTENSION RESULTS

ZONE		
1	Fingers more than 7.5cm (3in) apart	
2	Fingertips touch	
3	You can interlock your fingers	

A good range of movement around the shoulders is important for all racket sports
ZONE 1
You definitely need to do more stretching
ZONE 2
You are fairly flexible but should do more stretching
ZONE 3
You have good flexibility: stretch to maintain it

FORWARD FLEXION **Areas worked:** Lower back **Muscles used:** Erector spinae

1 Sit with your back straight, chest lifted and abdominals in.

2 Extend your legs to the sides in a comfortable V. Breathe in.

3 Breathe out as you slowly lean forward from your hips and lower

back and place your fists on the floor, one on top of the other.

4 Lower your chest toward your fists. Stop when you feel mild tension.

5 Measure the distance from the top of your top fist to your chest.

FORWARD FLEXION RESULTS

ZONE		
1	Chest more than 30cm (12in) from fist	
2	Chest reaches fist or within 5cm (2in)	
3	Chest at least 2.5cm (1in) lower than fist	

The lower back takes a good deal of the stress in lifting and impact sports
ZONE 1
You definitely need to do more stretching
ZONE 2
You are fairly flexible but should do more stretching
ZONE 3
You have good flexibility: stretch to maintain it

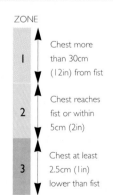

YOUR OVERALL ASSESSMENT

Now that you have all the results of your tests and know how fit you are, you can decide how best to proceed. Look again at your goals. Do they still appear to be realistic? If you can answer yes, you are almost on your way. (If the results of your endurance and strength tests are poor or fair, ask your doctor to confirm that you are fit enough to start exercising.)

If your goal is an overall improvement in your fitness level and your three test results show a wide discrepancy, postpone work on a menu until you have reached broadly the same level in all three categories. If you are intermediate in terms of strength and have good flexibility, for example, but are a poor beginner in endurance, follow one of the beginners' aerobic programmes for a few weeks, then repeat the test. You will probably now be ready to start on an intermediate menu. If your upper and middle body strength ratings are good but your lower body is poor, spend some time on beginners' leg strengtheners. Test yourself again and you may be ready to start on an intermediate or advanced menu.

Choose the menu that is appropriate to your fitness level. If you are under 35, you should be able to work through the menu with no trouble. If you are over 50, take things more slowly: work at about half the rate indicated, spending two weeks on each week's sessions. If you are between 35 and 50, do the first half of a programme or menu as it stands, then cut back to spending two weeks per week indicated.

If your major goal is aerobic fitness, follow the programme you think will suit you best, beginning at an appropriate level. Again, depending on your age, slow the pace at which you work through the programme, if necessary.

Don't lose sight of your goal but be realistic. If your tests point to an advanced programme but you can't cope, go back a few weeks into the intermediate suggestions. You will probably find that you make good progress (better to lose a month now than find the going so tough that you give up altogether).

PERSONAL TRAINER'S TIPS

Keeping a programme going isn't easy but these few pointers may help you.
- Be habitual: train at the same time of day and on the same days of the week so that fitness is part of your everyday life.
- Set several small goals to lead to your major one. Reward yourself (not with food) as you reach them.
- Don't worry if you fall back, simply keep going.
- If it gets tough you may find a partner helps.
- Be realistic: look at yourself in the mirror often and check that what you are trying to achieve is possible.
- Keep your programme varied: run instead of cycling one week; do a couple of circuits instead of a gym session and so on.

THE FOUR VARIABLES

All the menus and programmes are governed by four variables of exercise: frequency, intensity, duration and type.

Frequency is the number of sessions you work. The body needs rest between sessions to adapt to the higher demands being made on it. An occasional session is as bad as too many, however. Keep your workouts regular: three a week is ideal, with rest days in between.

Intensity is the effort you put into a workout. To achieve results, your body must work harder than normal. Your TTZ (see p. 21) offers the clearest indication that you are working hard enough to produce an improvement in fitness.

Duration of each session should be built up gradually. Don't exceed 2 hours per session. Time is complementary to intensity; be aware that most people spend too much time at too low an intensity.

Type of training depends on your goals: do you need to concentrate on a specific area or do you want a general fitness programme?

Finally, be realistic in your expectations. As you work through a menu, developing muscle and losing fat, your body shape will change. Work on your shoulders and back will give your upper body better proportions; work on your thighs may make your legs appear longer and leaner. You can't do anything about your body type (pp. 18–19).

EQUIPMENT

You don't need a great deal of equipment in order to do the majority of the exercises in this book. A workout bench is a good idea and, as you progress through the fitness levels, will become an essential; you do need a set of dumbbells (but not a barbell) at beginners' and intermediate levels. Everything else shown here is a matter of choice.

Buying equipment for use at home can be expensive: it is important to buy the best quality that you can afford. Before you buy anything, make sure that it is exactly what you are looking for, check that it meets your needs, make sure that you "fit" the piece (always opt for adjustable machines) and that you are going to be able to use it on your own. Are you sure you are going to use it regularly?

If you are buying large items such as an exercise bicycle (rather than an outdoor model) or rowing machine, look at various makes and models and ask for explanations of the differences between them (ask at the shop but also check with the instructors at a local gym or health club: they will be able to offer you impartial advice). Remember that the most expensive model is not necessarily going to suit you and your needs.

Many machines are sophisticated with computerized programming; try to buy equipment that is maintenance-free and always check the warranty for parts and labour in case you have problems later.

A Exercise bicycle: for use indoors; check that it is stable, adjustable and comfortable.

B Rowing machine: wide choice with many computerized to make training more fun.

C Step: choose one that is large enough to step on with comfort, hard-wearing and adjustable.
D Mat: useful for floor work, must be spongy and washable.

E Dumbbells: choose a set with discs so that you can adjust weight as necessary.
F Wrist weights.
G Personal alarm: essential for joggers.

H Pedometer: gives accurate distance measurements.
I Pulse monitor.
J Barbell: bars vary in length and weight, check before you buy.
K Block: raises feet to help keep back on bench.
L Ankle weights: buy those with individual weight bags.
M Trampoline: good for running in bad weather.
N Workout bench: must be sturdy and stable. Most are standard size so check you "fit". A rack is a good idea for use with free weights; do you need an incline setting?

CLOTHES

The most important factors when choosing clothes are that they should be comfortable and loose and that the fabrics should breathe. Clothes must also, obviously, be suitable for the activity.

It is not necessary to buy the latest fashions in sportswear but if you are going to engage in an activity more than twice a week, buy the best you can afford. Remember how often you are going to wash these items: good-quality clothes that wash well are worth the cost in the long term. You will need at least two sets of clothes for the week and always have an extra sweatshirt to hand.

Don't buy a complete sports wardrobe in one go. Buy the basics for your major activity and add to them as you progress (clothes are good rewards for reaching targets).

Finally, for women, a comfortable, supporting sports bra is a must.

INDOOR GEAR
Shorts and a vest are a good choice for indoor and the majority of outdoor work. Wear loose shorts for running.

A loose-fitting leotard with leggings or a unitard is ideal for indoor workouts. Lightweight socks are a must.

SWIMWEAR AND EQUIPMENT

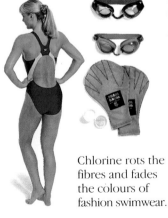

Nose and ear plugs are a good idea and goggles a must for swimming. A hat cuts down drag while webbed gloves allow you to use the water as a resistance.

Chlorine rots the fibres and fades the colours of fashion swimwear.

Buy swimwear designed for sports use which reduces drag in

the water and washes well; shoulder straps must be secure.

OUTDOOR GEAR

Wind- and waterproof jacket in a fabric that breathes is useful in changeable climates. If not hooded, wear a hat and scarf or towel in cold weather.

Gloves can be a good idea: hands should be relaxed which they will not be if too cold.

Warm tracksuit must be loose and comfortable.

T-shirt of cotton, the best fabric next to the skin.

Hooded top keeps neck warm and offers protection from wind.

Pockets hold keys, personal alarm and discarded gloves.

Lightweight trousers or shorts are ideal on warmer days.

Too many layers are better than too few for outdoor wear. It is always possible to take a sweatshirt off and wrap it round your waist. Always wear appropriate shoes (see pp. 34–35).

CYCLING GEAR

Cyclists need a well-fitting helmet (*left*) and goggles that cover the eye socket (*far left*). A water bottle is a must. Toe clips take your legs through their full range of movement. Wear sports-specific clothing, gloves and shoes.

SHOES

Training shoes absorb the impact of your feet on the ground, usually by means of layers of different materials embedded in the midsole; and they support your feet, through stabilizing straps, varying heel heights, and contoured sock liners or midsoles. These shoes are not cheap, but to work in unsuitable shoes is to court injury.

Cross trainers are ideal if you play tennis or badminton once a week, do an occasional aerobics class and some circuits: they are not suitable for frequent running. These shoes are designed for stability: their outer soles and treads do not have enough traction for regular running and other impact activities.

Running shoes must be specific: you can't run in anything else. Look for light, durable uppers in quick-drying fabric. They should also have high heels to avoid strain on your Achilles tendons and calves, with cushioning to absorb impact, and reflective strips for safety. Running shoes give no protection against roll, so are not suitable for racket sports.

Walking shoes need to flex at the ball of the foot, with the heel higher than the front of the shoe. Look, too, for stability and shock absorbency.

Look at the shock absorption and stabilizing features first, then consider comfort and durability. Check for a strong lacing system and uppers made from lightweight materials that breathe. Check, too, the height of the heel and counter and the width of the toe box.

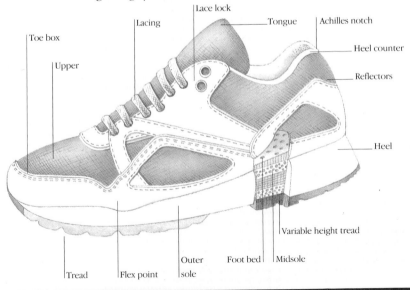

Toe box
Upper
Lacing
Lace lock
Tongue
Achilles notch
Heel counter
Reflectors
Heel
Variable height tread
Tread
Flex point
Outer sole
Foot bed
Midsole

Aerobics shoes must hold your feet firmly and should have shock absorbency under, and a flex point near, the ball of the foot.

Tennis shoes need lateral stabilizing straps, midsoles and outer soles that wrap over the uppers, and stiff heel counters. They must be durable, with a strong toe box.

Buy shoes at the end of the day when your feet have expanded. Try some of the movements you do when exercising. Don't expect new shoes to feel as comfortable as your old ones: shoes that are too soft to begin with won't keep their shape.

Running shoes need good shock absorbency in the midsole and under the heel.

To help in buying shoes, press your wet feet on a hard surface.

If your print shows more than half your feet (*top*) you have a low arch and instep. Buy shoes that offer stability first, then cushioning.

If your print shows half your foot (*centre*), most shoes are suitable.

If your print is small, you have a high arch. Buy shoes with good shock absorbency in the midsole first, then look for stability.

Lateral stabilizing straps across the laces help to hold your feet firmly in aerobics shoes.

Designed for stability, cross trainers have straps, supports and strong cushioning. They are becoming more sophisticated, with shoes balanced toward one activity. As your goals become specific, buy a pair geared toward your principal activity.

35

WARMING UP

Warming up and cooling down are integral parts of any workout or sport. A warm up prepares the body for the work to come by getting the cardiovascular system working efficiently (see pp. 12–13). This, in turn, allows the joints to start working freely which increases the flow of synovial fluid around them (see pp. 16–17), making them more pliable. A warm up should last 10–15 minutes and raise your pulse to 45–50% of its maximum, not into your TTZ (see p. 21).

If you suddenly stop work, your body goes into shock; the muscles contract and blood pools in the veins. This can cause dizziness or chest pains at the time and lactic acid build up, stiffness and loss of flexibility later. Cooling down slows your blood flow to normal gradually.

SIDE ARM REACH

Breathe normally throughout.

1 Stand with your back straight, chest lifted and abdominals in.

2 Place your feet more than shoulder width apart and bend your knees slightly.

3 With your right hand on your hip and left over your head, lift from the waist and lean to the right.

4 Hold briefly, then repeat with your right arm over your head and lean to your left.

ARM SWINGS

PHASE **1**
1 Stand as for a plié squat (see p. 84).

2 Cross your hands in front of your hips.

PHASE **2**
3 Take a deep breath in as you swing your arms out to your sides and up over your head.

4 Breathe out as you swing your arms back to the start position. Make the arm circle as large as you can.

5 Repeat continuously.

UP AND BACK REACH

Breathe normally throughout.

PHASE █
1 Stand with your back straight, chest lifted and abdominals in.

2 Place your feet hip width apart and bend your knees slightly.

3 Slowly extend your left arm straight up.

4 At the same time extend your right arm down and back: press as far back as is comfortable.

PHASE █
5 Hold briefly, then swap arms, swinging your right arm up and left arm down and back. Keep your back straight.

6 Repeat continuously.

SHOULDER ROLLS

Breathe normally throughout.

1 Stand with your back straight, chest lifted and abdominals in.

2 Place your feet hip width apart and bend your knees slightly.

3 Slowly and leading with your elbow, roll your right shoulder forward and up, then backward and down.

4 Repeat, this time taking your shoulder backward and down, then rolling it forward and up.

5 Repeat using your left arm.

6 Repeat working both arms at the same time.

WARM UP EXERCISES

Slow, smooth and rhythmic movements that imitate the activity that is going to be included in your session – running, swimming or cycling, for example – are ideal warm up exercises. All the cool down suggestions on pp. 38–39 can also be used. In addition, try the exercises on pp. 186–87. Remember to include short (8–10 second) stretches in your warm up.

COOLING DOWN

KNEE LIFT TURNOUT

Breathe normally throughout.

PHASE
1 Stand with your back straight, chest lifted and abdominals in.

2 Place your feet hip width apart and bend your knees slightly. Place your hands on your hips for balance.

3 Slowly raise your right knee in front of you. Stop when your thigh is parallel to the floor.

PHASE
4 Slowly, leading with the outside of your thigh, take your knee out to the right.

5 Hold briefly, then bring your knee back to the start position at the centre of your body.

6 Repeat using your left leg.

Note: You may find this exercise easier if you use a chair as support.

WAIST TWISTS

Breathe normally throughout.

PHASE ◼
1 Stand with your back straight, chest lifted and abdominals in.

2 Place your feet hip width apart and bend your knees slightly. Keep your head in line with your spine.

3 Extend both arms out directly in front of you at shoulder height.

PHASE ◼
4 Bend your right elbow and, leading with your elbow and keeping your hips square to the front, twist your upper body as far to the right as you can.

5 Twist back to the start position.

6 Repeat turning to your left.

SKI SWINGS

PHASE ▮

1 Stand with your back straight, chest lifted and abdominals pulled in.

2 Place your feet hip width apart and bend your knees slightly. Keep your head in line with your spine.

3 Extend both arms out in front of you at above shoulder height and breathe in.

PHASE ▮

4 Breathe out as you slowly bend at the hips and knees and sweep downward with both arms.

5 Continue the sweep until both arms are behind you. Don't exceed your range of movement.

6 Hold briefly, then breathe in as you sweep your arms back to the start position. Keep your heels on the floor and press up through your hips and knees.

7 Repeat continuously.

HOPSCOTCH

Breathe normally throughout.

1 Stand with your back straight, chest lifted and abdominals in.

2 Place your feet hip width apart and bend your knees slightly. Keep your hips square to the front.

3 Press your right heel to your left buttock, then left heel to your right buttock.

4 When you have this movement working easily and smoothly, start to work your arms too.

5 Touch your right foot with your left hand and left foot with your right hand. Keep your back straight and abdominals in.

COOL DOWN EXERCISES

As with warming up, slow rhythmic movements that mimic the activity you have been working, such as cycling or jogging, are suitable as cool down exercises. All the warm up exercises on pp. 36–37 are also good cool down activities. In addition, try the exercises on pp. 186–87. Remember to include developmental (20–30 second) stretches in your cool down.

BEGINNERS • Men

The beginners' menu works the whole body in the three basic areas of fitness: aerobic endurance, strength (both "pure" strength and muscular endurance) and flexibility.

Before you begin, read the information below and **Into the menu** on p. 42.

How to proceed Take a photocopy of the scorecard on p. 217: this will allow you to keep a week-by-week record of your progress. Fill in the list of exercises given here, taking the sets and reps for the strength exercises from the pages indicated.

The exercises are listed in the order in which you should do them. This is so that you do not work exercises for the same body part one after the other, which can quickly lead to muscle fatigue.

Remember: The "right" weight is one that makes the last couple of reps a challenge to complete – 1kg (2¼lb) is the most appropriate at this level.

WEEKS 1–2
Twice a week
Warm up
(pp. 36–37) and short (8–10 second) stretches for all major muscle groups, pp. 150–83
For endurance
5 minutes any aerobic activity, pp. 58–73
For strength
Squats, p. 80 Press ups – wall, p. 102 Lower back raises, p. 114 Single arm crunches, p. 142
Cool down
(pp. 38–39) and, for flexibility, developmental (20–30 second) stretches for the whole body

WEEKS 3–4
Twice a week
Warm up
(pp. 36–37) and short (8–10 second) stretches for all major muscle groups, pp. 150–83
For endurance
10 minutes any aerobic activity, pp. 58–73
For strength
Squats, p. 80 Press ups – wall, p. 102 Lower back raises, p. 114 Dumbbell curls, p. 130 Single arm crunches, p. 142
Cool down
(pp. 38–39) and, for flexibility, developmental (20–30 second) stretches for the whole body

Squats, p. 80

WEEKS 5–6

Three times a week

Warm up

(pp. 36–37) and short
(8–10 second) stretches
for all major muscle
groups, pp. 150–83

For endurance

13 minutes any aerobic
activity, pp. 58–73

For strength

Squats, p. 80
Press ups – wall, p. 102
Lower back raises, p. 114
Dumbbell curls, p. 130
Triceps dips, p. 138
Single arm crunches, p. 142

Cool down

(pp. 38–39) and, for
flexibility, developmental
(20–30 second) stretches
for the whole body

WEEKS 7–8

Three times a week

Warm up

(pp. 36–37) and short
(8–10 second) stretches
for all major muscle
groups, pp. 150–83

For endurance

16 minutes any aerobic
activity, pp. 58–73

For strength

Squats, p. 80
Press ups – wall, p. 102
Lower back raises, p. 114
Dumbbell curls, p. 130
Triceps dips, p. 138
Single arm crunches, p. 142
Twists, p. 147

Cool down

(pp. 38–39) and, for
flexibility, developmental
(20–30 second) stretches
for the whole body

WEEKS 9–10

Three times a week

Warm up

(pp. 36–37) and short
(8–10 second) stretches
for all major muscle
groups, pp. 150–83

For endurance

20 minutes any aerobic
activity, pp. 58–73

For strength

Squats, p. 80
Press ups – wall, p. 102
Lower back raises, p. 114
Dumbbell curls, p. 130
Triceps dips, p. 138
Calf raises, p. 100
Single arm crunches, p. 142
Twists, p. 147

Cool down

(pp. 38–39) and, for
flexibility, developmental
(20–30 second) stretches
for the whole body

BEGINNERS • Women

The beginners' menu works the whole body in the three basic areas of fitness: aerobic endurance, strength (both "pure" strength and muscular endurance) and flexibility.

Before you begin, read the information below and the section entitled **How to proceed** on p. 40.

What to expect It is a fact that women carry more body fat than men and you may find that your shape is not changing as fast as you would like. Don't despair. Do plenty of aerobic work between your workouts and take care over your diet.

Into the menu If you find after week 2 that the work is difficult, don't proceed to week 3; conversely if at the end of week 6, it all seems rather easy, try the menu for weeks 1–2 of the intermediate programme.

Remember: The "right" weight is one that makes the last couple of reps a challenge to complete – 1kg (2¼lb) is the most appropriate at this level.

WEEKS 1–2
Twice a week
Warm up
(pp. 36–37) and short (8–10 second) stretches for all major muscle groups, pp. 150–83
For endurance
5 minutes any aerobic activity, pp. 58–73
For strength
Lunges, p. 78   Press ups – wall, p. 102   Lower back raises, p. 114   Single arm crunches, p. 142
Cool down
(pp. 38–39) and, for flexibility, developmental (20–30 second) stretches for the whole body

WEEKS 3–4
Twice a week
Warm up
(pp. 36–37) and short (8–10 second) stretches for all major muscle groups, pp. 150–83
For endurance
10 minutes any aerobic activity, pp. 58–75
For strength
Lunges, p. 78   Press ups – wall, p. 102   Inner thigh raises, p. 92   Lower back raises, p. 114   Single arm crunches, p. 142
Cool down
(pp. 38–39) and, for flexibility, developmental (20–30 second) stretches for the whole body

Lunges, p. 78

WEEKS 5–6

Three times a week

Warm up

(pp. 36–37) and short
(8–10 second) stretches
for all major muscle
groups, pp. 150–83

For endurance

13 minutes any aerobic
activity, pp. 58–73

For strength

Lunges, p. 78
Press ups – wall, p. 102
Inner thigh raises, p. 92
Lower back raises, p. 114
Triceps dips, p. 138
Single arm crunches, p. 142

Cool down

(pp. 38–39) and, for
flexibility, developmental
(20–30 second) stretches
for the whole body

WEEKS 7–8

Three times a week

Warm up

(pp. 36–37) and short
(8–10 second) stretches
for all major muscle
groups, pp. 150–83

For endurance

16 minutes any aerobic
activity, pp. 58–73

For strength

Lunges, p. 78
Press ups – wall, p. 102
Inner thigh raises, p. 92
Lower back raises, p. 114
Calf raises, p. 100
Dumbbell curls, p. 130
Triceps dips, p. 138
Single arm crunches, p. 142

Cool down

(pp. 38–39) and, for
flexibility, developmental
(20–30 second) stretches
for the whole body

WEEKS 9–10

Three times a week

Warm up

(pp. 36–37) and short
(8–10 second) stretches
for all major muscle
groups, pp. 150–83

For endurance

20 minutes any aerobic
activity, pp. 58–73

For strength

Lunges, p. 78
Press ups – wall, p. 102
Inner thigh raises, p. 92
Lower back raises, p. 114
Calf raises, p. 100
Dumbbell curls, p. 130
Triceps dips, p. 138
Single arm crunches, p. 142
Twists, p. 147

Cool down

(pp. 38–39) and, for
flexibility, developmental
(20–30 second) stretches
for the whole body

INTERMEDIATE • Men

If you are starting your fitness programme at this level, read the information entitled **How to proceed** on p. 40 before you begin. **Structuring a workout** At this level, the list of exercises starts to get longer and it becomes vital not to work exercises for the same body part one after another. You should, therefore, work the exercises in the order in which they are listed here. Where consecutive exercises are for the same body part, they are working different muscles. The exercises are also structured so that you work the larger muscle groups before the smaller ones to be sure that the smaller groups get enough oxygen to work properly.

If this menu is too easy or too difficult, read **Into the menu** on p. 46.

Remember: The "right" weight is one that makes the last couple of reps a challenge – 2–3kg (4½–6¾lb) is the most appropriate at this level.

WEEKS 1–2	WEEKS 3–4
Three times a week	Three times a week
Warm up	**Warm up**
(pp. 36–37) and short (8–10 second) stretches for all major muscle groups, pp. 150–83	(pp. 36–37) and short (8–10 second) stretches for all major muscle groups, pp. 150–83
For endurance	**For endurance**
10 minutes any aerobic activity, pp. 58–73	15 minutes any aerobic activity, pp. 58–73
For strength	**For strength**
Squats, p. 81 Press ups – box, p. 103 Lower back raises, p. 115 Dumbbell curls, p. 130 Triceps dips, p. 138 Lateral raises, p. 105 Crunches, p. 141 Twists, p. 147	Squats, p. 81 Press ups – box, p. 103 Calf raises, p. 101 Lower back raises, p. 115 Dumbbell curls, p. 130 Triceps dips, p. 138 Lateral raises, p. 105 Crunches, p. 141 Twists, p. 147
Cool down	**Cool down**
(pp. 38–39) and, for flexibility, developmental (20–30 second) stretches for the whole body	(pp. 38–39) and, for flexibility, developmental (20–30 second) stretches for the whole body

Lunges, p. 78

WEEKS 5–6

Three times a week

Warm up

(pp. 36–37) and short
(8–10 second) stretches
for all major muscle
groups, pp. 150–83

For endurance

20 minutes any aerobic
activity, pp. 58–73

For strength

Squats, p. 81
Press ups – box, p. 103
Calf raises, p. 101
Lower back raises, p. 115
Dumbbell curls, p. 130
Triceps dips, p. 138
Lateral raises, p. 105
Crunches, p. 141
Twists, p. 147

Cool down

(pp. 38–39) and, for
flexibility, developmental
(20–30 second) stretches
for the whole body

WEEKS 7–8

Three times a week

Warm up

(pp. 36–37) and short
(8–10 second) stretches
for all major muscle
groups, pp. 150–83

For endurance

25 minutes any aerobic
activity, pp. 58–73

For strength

Lunges, p. 78
Press ups – box, p. 103
Calf raises, p. 101
Lower back raises, p. 115
Single arm rows, p. 116
Dumbbell curls, p. 130
Triceps dips, p. 138
Lateral raises, p. 105
Crunches, p. 141
Twists, p. 147

Cool down

(pp. 38–39) and, for
flexibility, developmental
(20–30 second) stretches
for the whole body

WEEKS 9–10

Three times a week

Warm up

(pp. 36–37) and short
(8–10 second) stretches
for all major muscle
groups, pp.150–83

For endurance

30 minutes any aerobic
activity, pp. 58–73

For strength

Lunges, p. 78
Press ups – box, p. 103
Calf raises, p. 101
Lower back raises, p. 115
Single arm rows, p. 116
Dumbbell curls, p. 130
Triceps dips, p. 138
Lateral raises, p. 105
Bench presses, pp. 124–25
Crunches, p. 141
Twists, p. 147

Cool down

(pp. 38–39) and, for
flexibility, developmental
(20–30 second) stretches
for the whole body

INTERMEDIATE • Women

If you are starting your fitness programme at this level, read **How to proceed** on p. 40 and the details on **Structuring a workout** on p. 44.

Using weights Many women worry about working with weights. At this level you will be using light weights which will not give you a body builder's physique: for that you would have to work out 2–4 hours a day using heavy weights.

Into the menu If you start at this level and find it difficult, try weeks 7–8 of the beginners' menu to see if you find that easier to sustain. Do weeks 9–10 of that menu then try the intermediate again. You may be surprised at the ease with which you complete it now.

If, at the end of week 6, this menu seems too easy, try the advanced menu.

Remember: The "right" weight is one that makes the last couple of reps a challenge – 2–3kg (4½–6¾lb) is the most appropriate at this level.

WEEKS 1–2
Three times a week
Warm up
(pp. 36–37) and short (8–10 second) stretches for all major muscle groups, pp. 150–83
For endurance
10 minutes any aerobic activity, pp. 58–73
For strength
Lunges, p. 78
Press ups – box, p. 103
Inner thigh raises, p. 93
Lower back raises, p. 115
Calf raises, p. 101
Dumbbell curls, p. 130
Triceps dips, p. 138
Crunches, p. 141
Twists, p. 147
Cool down
(pp. 38–39) and, for flexibility, developmental (20–30 second) stretches for the whole body

WEEKS 3–4
Three times a week
Warm up
(pp. 36–37) and short (8–10 second) stretches for all major muscle groups, pp. 150–83
For endurance
15 minutes any aerobic activity, pp. 58–73
For strength
Lunges, p. 78
Press ups – box, p. 103
Inner thigh raises, p. 93
Lower back raises, p. 115
Calf raises, p. 101
Shoulder presses, p. 107
Dumbbell curls, p. 130
Triceps dips, p. 138
Crunches, p. 141
Twists, p. 147
Cool down
(pp. 38–39) and, for flexibility, developmental (20–30 second) stretches for the whole body

Box press ups, p. 103

WEEKS 5–6

Three times a week

Warm up

(pp. 36–37) and short
(8–10 second) stretches
for all major muscle
groups, pp. 150–83

For endurance

20 minutes any aerobic
activity, pp. 58–73

For strength

Lunges, p. 78
Press ups – box, p. 103
Inner thigh raises, p. 93
Lower back raises, p. 115
Calf raises, p. 101
Shoulder presses, p. 107
Dumbbell curls, p. 130
Triceps dips, p. 138
Crunches, p. 141
Twists, p. 147

Cool down

(pp. 38–39) and, for
flexibility, developmental
(20–30 second) stretches
for the whole body

WEEKS 7–8

Three times a week

Warm up

(pp. 36–37) and short
(8–10 second) stretches
for all major muscle
groups, pp. 150–83

For endurance

25 minutes any aerobic
activity, pp. 58–73

For strength

Lunges, p. 78
Press ups – box, p. 103
Inner thigh raises, p. 93
Lower back raises, p. 115
Calf raises, p. 101
Shoulder presses, p. 107
Lateral raises, p. 105
Dumbbell curls, p. 130
Triceps dips, p. 138
Crunches, p. 141
Twists, p. 147

Cool down

(pp. 38–39) and, for
flexibility, developmental
(20–30 second) stretches
for the whole body

WEEKS 9–10

Three times a week

Warm up

(pp. 36–37) and short
(8–10 second) stretches
for all major muscle
groups, pp. 150–83

For endurance

30 minutes any aerobic
activity, pp. 58–73

For strength

Lunges, p. 78
Press ups – box, p. 103
Inner thigh raises, p. 93
Lower back raises, p. 115
Calf raises, p. 101
Shoulder presses, p. 107
Lateral raises, p. 105
Dumbbell curls, p. 130
Triceps dips, p. 138
Crunches, p. 141
Twists, p. 147
Lower abdomen
raises, p. 145

Cool down

(pp. 38–39) and, for
flexibility, developmental
(20–30 second) stretches
for the whole body

ADVANCED • Men

If you are starting your fitness programme at this level, first read **How to proceed** on p. 40 and **Structuring a workout** on p. 44. Also read **When to train** on p. 50.

Coping with plateaus
As the list of exercises becomes longer and the sessions more taxing, you may hit a plateau: you stop seeing any progress no matter how hard you work. Don't get disheartened. If you stay on a programme for too long it is natural that both body and mind become stale. If this happens, change your routine slightly. Either increase the weight and reduce the reps, or lower the weight and increase the reps.

Remember: The "right" weight is one that makes the last couple of reps a challenge.

WEEKS 1–2	WEEKS 3–4
Three times a week	Three times a week
Warm up	**Warm up**
(pp. 36–37) and short (8–10 second) stretches for all major muscle groups, pp. 150–83	(pp. 36–37) and short (8–10 second) stretches for all major muscle groups, pp. 150–83
For endurance	**For endurance**
20 minutes any aerobic activity, pp. 58–73	25 minutes any aerobic activity, pp. 58–73
For strength	**For strength**
Lunges, p. 79 Press ups – ¾, p. 104 Calf raises, p. 101 Lower back raises, p. 115 Bench presses, p. 124 Single arm rows, p. 116 Lateral raises, p. 105 Dumbbell curls, p. 130 Triceps kickbacks, p. 135 Crunches, p. 141 Twists, p. 147	Lunges, p. 79 Press ups – ¾, p. 104 Calf raises, p. 101 Lower back raises, p. 115 Bench presses, p. 124 Single arm rows, p. 116 Lateral raises, p. 105 Forward raises, p. 111 Dumbbell curls, p. 130 Triceps kickbacks, p. 135 Crunches, p. 141 Twists, p. 147
Cool down	**Cool down**
(pp. 38–39) and, for flexibility, developmental (20–30 second) stretches for the whole body	(pp. 38–39) and, for flexibility, developmental (20–30 second) stretches for the whole body

Three-quarter
press ups, p. 104

WEEKS 5–6

Three times a week

Warm up

(pp. 36–37) and short
(8–10 second) stretches
for all major muscle
groups, pp. 150–83

For endurance

30 minutes any aerobic
activity, pp. 58–73

For strength

Lunges, p. 79
Press ups – ¾, p. 104
Calf raises, p. 101
Lower back raises, p. 115
Bench presses, p. 124
Single arm rows, p. 116
Lateral raises, p. 105
Forward raises, p. 111
Shoulder presses, p. 107
Dumbbell curls, p. 130
Triceps kickbacks, p. 135
Crunches, p. 141
Twists, p. 147

Cool down

(pp. 38–39) and, for
flexibility, developmental
(20–30 second) stretches
for the whole body

WEEKS 7–8

Three times a week

Warm up

(pp. 36–37) and short
(8–10 second) stretches
for all major muscle
groups, pp. 150–83

For endurance

35 minutes any aerobic
activity, pp. 58–73

For strength

Lunges, p. 79
Press ups – ¾, p. 104
Calf raises, p. 101
Lower back raises, p. 115
Bench presses, p. 124
Single arm rows, p. 116
Lateral raises, p. 105
Forward raises, p. 111
Shoulder presses, p. 107
Dumbbell curls, p. 130
Triceps kickbacks, p. 135
Crunches, p. 141
Twists, p. 147

Cool down

(pp. 38–39) and, for
flexibility, developmental
(20–30 second) stretches
for the whole body

WEEKS 9–10

Three times a week

Warm up

(pp. 36–37) and short
(8–10 second) stretches
for all major muscle
groups, pp. 150–83

For endurance

40 minutes any aerobic
activity, pp. 58–73

For strength

Lunges, p. 79
Press ups – ¾, p. 104
Calf raises, p. 101
Lower back raises, p. 115
Bench presses, p. 124
Single arm rows, p. 116
Press behind
neck, p. 108
Lateral raises, p. 105
Forward raises, p. 111
Shoulder presses, p. 107
Dumbbell curls, p. 130
Triceps kickbacks, p. 135
Concentrated curls, p. 131
Knee raised
crunches, p. 146

Cool down

(pp. 38–39) and, for
flexibility, developmental
(20–30 second) stretches
for the whole body

ADVANCED • Women

If you are starting your fitness programme at this level, first read **How to proceed** on p. 40 and **Structuring a workout** on p. 44.

When to train At this level, you may wish to do your aerobics work on the same days as your weight training. If you do, try to do one in the morning and the other in the evening. If you can't, do your aerobics first as this will not diminish your lifting power. If you weight train first you may be too tired for a 20–30 minute aerobics session as well.

You may also find the information on **Coping with plateaus** on p. 48 useful.

Remember: The "right" weight is one that makes the last couple of reps a challenge.

WEEKS 1–2
Three times a week
Warm up
(pp. 36–37) and short (8–10 second) stretches for all major muscle groups, pp. 150–83
For endurance
20 minutes any aerobic activity, pp. 58–73
For strength
Squats, p. 82
Press ups – ¾, p. 104
Inner thigh raises, p. 94
Lower back raises, p. 115
Calf raises, p. 101
Shoulder presses, p. 107
Lateral raises, p. 105
Dumbbell curls, p. 130
Triceps dips, p. 138
Crunches, p. 141
Twists, p. 147
Lower abdomen raises, p. 145
Cool down
(pp. 38–39) and, for flexibility, developmental (20–30 second) stretches for the whole body

WEEKS 3–4
Three times a week
Warm up
(pp. 36–37) and short (8–10 second) stretches for all major muscle groups, pp. 150–83
For endurance
25 minutes any aerobic activity, pp. 58–73
For strength
Squats, p. 82
Press ups – ¾, p. 104
Inner thigh raises, p. 94
Lower back raises, p. 115
Calf raises, p. 101
Flat bench flies, p. 127
Shoulder presses, p. 107
Lateral raises, p. 105
Dumbbell curls, p. 130
Triceps dips, p. 138
Crunches, p. 141
Twists, p. 147
Lower abdomen raises, p. 145
Cool down
(pp. 38–39) and, for flexibility, developmental (20–30 second) stretches for the whole body

Lower back raises, p. 115

WEEKS 5–6	WEEKS 7–8	WEEKS 9–10
Three times a week	Three times a week	Three times a week

Warm up

(pp. 36–37) and short (8–10 second) stretches for all major muscle groups, pp. 150–83

For endurance

30 minutes any aerobic activity, pp. 58–73

For strength

Squats, p. 82
Press ups – ¾, p. 104
Inner thigh raises, p. 94
Lower back raises, p. 115
Calf raises, p. 101
Flat bench flies, p. 127
Shoulder presses, p. 107
Lateral raises, p. 105
Dumbbell curls, p. 130
Triceps dips, p. 138
Crunches, p. 141
Twists, p. 147
Lower abdomen raises, p. 145

Cool down

(pp. 38–39) and, for flexibility, developmental (20–30 second) stretches for the whole body

---

Warm up

(pp. 36–37) and short (8–10 second) stretches for all major muscle groups, pp. 150–83

For endurance

35 minutes any aerobic activity, pp. 58–73

For strength

Squats, p. 82
Press ups – ¾, p. 104
Inner thigh raises, p. 94
Lower back raises, p. 115
Calf raises, p. 101
Flat bench flies, p. 127
Upright rows, p. 110
Shoulder presses, p. 107
Lateral raises, p. 105
Dumbbell curls, p. 130
Triceps dips, p. 138
Crunches, p. 141
Twists, p. 147
Lower abdomen raises, p. 145

Cool down

(pp. 38–39) and, for flexibility, developmental (20–30 second) stretches for the whole body

---

Warm up

(pp. 36–37) and short (8–10 second) stretches for all major muscle groups, pp. 150–83

For endurance

40 minutes any aerobic activity, pp. 58–73

For strength

Squats, p. 82
Press ups – ¾, p. 104
Inner thigh raises, p. 94
Lower back raises, p. 115
Calf raises, p. 101
Bottom raises, p. 98
Upright rows, p. 110
Flat bench flies, p. 127
Single arm rows, p. 116
Shoulder presses, p. 107
Lateral raises, p. 105
Forward raises, p. 111
Dumbbell curls, p. 130
Triceps kickbacks, p. 135
Double crunches, p. 144

Cool down

(pp. 38–39) and, for flexibility, developmental (20–30 second) stretches for the whole body

EXPERT • Men

By the time you reach expert level, you will be sufficiently in tune with your body's capabilities to experiment with different types of routine, particularly in your strength work.

Pyramiding involves working different numbers of reps per set, such as 6–8–10–15 or 15–10–8–6.

Supersetting can be worked in two ways. In the first, you work the same body part using two exercises for antagonistic muscles, such as leg extensions followed by hamstring curls, so that while one muscle is working the other rests. This reduces the overall time of a session.

Alternatively, work one set of several exercises for the same muscle group in rapid succession: lat pull downs, seated rows and barbell rows.

Work sets of 8–10 reps with little or no rest between sets and/or exercises.

Further variations in training methods are given on p. 54.

52

WEEKS 1–2
Three times a week
Warm up
(pp. 36–37) and short (8–10 second) stretches for all major muscle groups, pp. 150–83
For endurance
30 minutes any aerobic activity, pp. 58–73
For strength
Lunges, p. 79
Calf raises, p. 101
Upright rows, p. 110
Bench presses, p. 124
Single arm rows, p. 116
Flat bench flies, p. 127
Lateral raises, p. 105
Shoulder presses, p. 107
Forward raises, p. 111
Lying elbow extensions, p. 139
Dumbbell curls, p. 130
Triceps kickbacks, p. 135
Concentrated curls, p. 131
Knee raised crunches, p. 146
Cool down
(pp. 38–39) and, for flexibility, developmental (20–30 second) stretches for the whole body

WEEKS 3–4
Three times a week
Warm up
(pp. 36–37) and short (8–10 second) stretches for all major muscle groups, pp. 150–83
For endurance
35 minutes any aerobic activity, pp. 58–73
For strength
Squats, p. 83
Calf raises, p. 101
Upright rows, p. 110
Bench presses, p. 124
Single arm rows, p. 116
Flat bench flies, p. 127
Lateral raises, p. 105
Shoulder presses, p. 107
Forward raises, p. 111
Press behind neck, p. 108
Lying elbow extensions, p. 139
Dumbbell curls, p. 130
Triceps kickbacks, p. 135
Concentrated curls, p. 131
Double crunches, p. 144
Cool down
(pp. 38–39) and, for flexibility, developmental (20–30 second) stretches for the whole body

WEEKS 5–6

Three times a week

Warm up

(pp. 36–37) and short
(8–10 second) stretches
for all major muscle
groups, pp. 150–83

For endurance

40 minutes any aerobic
activity, pp. 58–73

For strength

Squats, p. 83
Leg extensions, p. 87
Hamstring curls, p. 90
Calf raises, p. 101
Upright rows, p. 110
Bench presses, p. 124
Single arm rows, p. 116
Flat bench flies, p. 127
Lateral raises, p. 105
Shoulder presses, p. 107
Forward raises, p. 111
Press behind neck, p. 108
Lying elbow
extensions, p. 139
Dumbbell curls, p. 130
Triceps kickbacks, p. 135
Concentrated curls, p. 131
Double crunches, p. 144

Cool down

(pp. 38–39) and, for
flexibility, developmental
(20–30 second) stretches
for the whole body

WEEKS 7–8

Three times a week

Warm up

(pp. 36–37) and short
(8–10 second) stretches
for all major muscle
groups, pp. 150–83

For endurance

45 minutes any aerobic
activity, pp. 58–73

For strength

Squats, p. 83
Leg extensions, p. 87
Hamstring curls, p. 90
Calf raises, p. 101
Upright rows, p. 110
Bench presses, p. 124
Single arm rows, p. 116
Flat bench flies, p. 127
Lateral raises, p. 105
Shoulder presses, p. 107
Forward raises, p. 111
Press behind neck, p. 108
Lying elbow
extensions, p. 139
Dumbbell curls, p. 130
Triceps kickbacks, p. 135
Concentrated curls, p. 131
Double crunches, p. 144

Cool down

(pp. 38–39) and, for
flexibility, developmental
(20–30 second) stretches
for the whole body

WEEKS 9–10

Three times a week

Warm up

(pp. 36–37) and short
(8–10 second) stretches
for all major muscle
groups, pp. 150–83

For endurance

50 minutes any aerobic
activity, pp. 58–73

For strength

Squats, p. 83
Leg extensions, p. 87
Hamstring curls, p. 90
Calf raises, p. 101
Upright rows, p. 110
Bench presses, p. 124
Single arm rows, p. 116
Flat bench flies, p. 127
Lateral raises, p. 105
Shoulder presses, p. 107
Forward raises, p. 111
Bent forward laterals, p. 109
Press behind neck, p. 108
Lying elbow
extensions, p. 139
Dumbbell curls, p. 130
Triceps kickbacks, p. 135
Concentrated curls, p. 131
Double crunches, p. 144

Cool down

(pp. 38–39) and, for
flexibility, developmental
(20–30 second) stretches
for the whole body

EXPERT • Women

At expert level, the strength exercises you should work are many and time consuming. It becomes difficult to work hard enough in a single session to reap the benefits to each body part. The suggestions on p. 52 may help in reducing the time a session takes; you could also consider working split routines.

Split routines involve working the same body part on alternate days. A typical split routine is to train abdomen, arms and legs, for example, on Mondays, Wednesdays and Fridays, and back, chest and shoulders on Tuesdays, Thursdays and Saturdays. This system solves the time problem but it does of course mean that you are training virtually every day.

If you can't do that, put the exercises together in a way that reduces the sessions to four or five per week, but make sure that you don't work the same body part on consecutive days.

WEEKS 1–2	WEEKS 3–4
Three times a week	Three times a week
Warm up	**Warm up**
(pp. 36–37) and short (8–10 second) stretches for all major muscle groups, pp. 150–83	(pp. 36–37) and short (8–10 second) stretches for all major muscle groups, pp. 150–83
For endurance	**For endurance**
30 minutes any aerobic activity, pp. 58–73	35 minutes any aerobic activity, pp. 58–73
For strength	**For strength**
Squats, p. 83 Inner thigh raises, p. 94 Calf raises, p. 101 Press ups – full, p. 104 Upright rows, p. 110 Flat bench flies, p. 127 Single arm rows, p. 116 Shoulder presses, p. 107 Lateral raises, p. 105 Forward raises, p. 111 Dumbbell curls, p. 130 Triceps kickbacks, p. 135 Triceps extensions, p. 136 Double crunches, p. 144 Twists, p. 147	Lunges, p. 79 Inner thigh raises, p. 94 Calf raises, p. 101 Leg extensions, p. 87 Hamstring curls, p. 90 Upright rows, p. 110 Flat bench flies, p. 127 Single arm rows, p. 116 Shoulder presses, p. 107 Lateral raises, p. 105 Forward raises, p. 111 Dumbbell curls, p. 130 Triceps kickbacks, p. 135 Triceps extensions, p. 136 Double crunches, p. 144 Twists, p. 147
Cool down	**Cool down**
(pp. 38–39) and, for flexibility, developmental (20–30 second) stretches for the whole body	(pp. 38–39) and, for flexibility, developmental (20–30 second) stretches for the whole body

WEEKS 5–6

Three times a week

Warm up

(pp. 36–37) and short
(8–10 second) stretches
for all major muscle
groups, pp. 150–83

For endurance

40 minutes any aerobic
activity, pp. 58–73

For strength

Lunges, p. 79
Inner thigh raises, p. 94
Calf raises, p. 101
Leg extensions, p. 87
Hamstring curls, p. 90
Upright rows, p. 110
Flat bench flies, p. 127
Single arm rows, p. 116
Shoulder presses, p. 107
Lateral raises, p. 105
Forward raises, p. 111
Dumbbell curls, p. 130
Triceps kickbacks, p. 135
Concentrated curls, p. 131
Triceps extensions, p. 136
Double crunches, p. 144
Twists, p. 147

Cool down

(pp. 38–39) and, for
flexibility, developmental
(20–30 second) stretches
for the whole body

WEEKS 7–8

Three times a week

Warm up

(pp. 36–37) and short
(8–10 second) stretches
for all major muscle
groups, pp. 150–83

For endurance

45 minutes any aerobic
activity, pp. 58–73

For strength

Lunges, p. 79
Inner thigh raises, p. 94
Calf raises, p. 101
Leg extensions, p. 87
Hamstring curls, p. 90
Upright rows, p. 110
Flat bench flies, p. 127
Single arm rows, p. 116
Incline bench presses, p. 126
Shoulder presses, p. 107
Lateral raises, p. 105
Forward raises, p. 111
Dumbbell curls, p. 130
Triceps kickbacks, p. 135
Concentrated curls, p. 131
Triceps extensions, p. 136
Double crunches, p. 144
Twists, p. 147

Cool down

(pp. 38–39) and, for
flexibility, developmental
(20–30 second) stretches
for the whole body

WEEKS 9–10

Three times a week

Warm up

(pp. 36–37) and short
(8–10 second) stretches
for all major muscle
groups, pp. 150–83

For endurance

50 minutes any aerobic
activity, pp. 58–73

For strength

Lunges, p. 79
Inner thigh raises, p. 94
Calf raises, p. 101
Leg extensions, p. 87
Hamstring curls, p. 90
Upright rows, p. 110
Flat bench flies, p. 127
Single arm rows, p. 116
Incline bench presses, p. 126
Bent arm
pullovers, p. 129
Shoulder presses, p. 107
Lateral raises, p. 105
Forward raises, p. 111
Dumbbell curls, p. 130
Triceps kickbacks, p. 135
Concentrated curls, p. 131
Triceps extensions, p. 136
Double crunches, p. 144
Twists, p. 147

Cool down

(pp. 38–39) and, for
flexibility, developmental
(20–30 second) stretches
for the whole body

ENDURANCE • Introduction

There are two forms of endurance training: aerobic endurance and muscular endurance. Muscular endurance is discussed on pp. 74–75; this section is concerned primarily with aerobic endurance.

Aerobic exercise is the key to, and provides the solid foundation for, improving and maintaining your fitness and raising the quality of your life. There are several means of aerobic conditioning: the "big three" in terms of popularity at least are running, cycling and swimming. Power walking is the best way to start if you want to run eventually: if your current fitness level is low, you will find the running programme tough if you have not first completed the walking programme.

The cycling and running programmes are designed to be interchangeable. You can also alternate them with aerobic dance, skipping, rowing and circuit training (see pp. 184–89) to suit your individual needs.

The first result of aerobic work is that it improves your cardiovascular system (see also pp. 12–13). Aerobic training boosts your metabolism and, so long as you are also eating healthily (see pp. 204–9), offers the only safe and effective way to remove body fat. Aerobic exercise makes you feel good, although as with all forms of training and all bodyshaping and toning plans, it is a gradual process and hard work.

CLASSES: PROS AND CONS

Keeping to a fitness programme is difficult. With aerobic training, however, you do have the option of joining a class. Ten years ago, "aerobics" meant scores of people in a large room jumping up and down mechanically. Today, however, there are many safe, effective variations on the aerobics theme.

To have any effect, without causing injury, an aerobics class should last between 45 minutes and an hour; those that are longer are really only for the very fit. During the hour there should be an adequate warm up (suitable for your fitness level), which should include short (8–10 second) stretches. The aerobic section should last between 20 and 45 minutes, again depending on your fitness level.

During this period your heart should be working in its TTZ (see p. 21). The end of the session should include either an aerobic cool down or some strength or muscular endurance work, such as press ups or abdominal exercises. In both cases, there should then be a session of developmental (20–30 second) stretches for all the muscles groups.

You may have to try a few classes before you find one that suits you. The most common problems are: the music, which may be too fast, too loud, or simply something you hate; and the teacher, who may have put the workout together without taking account of the fitness levels of the group so that a limited few benefit from the session.

TYPES OF CLASSES
High-impact aerobics classes are energetic, with running and plyometrics (different exercises, all involving jumping). This means that at several points during the workout, both feet leave the floor, thereby causing "high-impact" as you land. These workouts are fun but they are not for you if you are starting out on a programme; nor are they suitable if you have lower back or knee problems and/or weak quadriceps and hamstrings.

Low-impact aerobics are ideal for beginners and experts alike. The moves are slower and more controlled, so that your posture remains good throughout. At any time one foot is always in contact with the floor, which puts less stress on your joints.

Step aerobics are also usually low impact and many people find that these classes suit them best since they are not too dance orientated. If you don't want to work step in a class situation, buy one of the many excellent videos for home use. Check the reviews in health and fitness magazines for the most suitable.

Circuit aerobics are great fun and involve working a circuit (see pp. 184–85) comprising several different aerobic activities to music.

Whichever class you choose, make sure that the teacher is qualified and that the programme is suited to your needs. Remember, too, that as you get fitter you will have to do more (an extra, longer or more intense session) to sustain improvements in your fitness level.

ENDURANCE • Walking

Fast walking, also known as brisk walking, power walking, fitness walking and power striding, is an underrated form of aerobic exercise. It is suitable for everyone, but particularly valuable for those who have problems with running and other high-impact activities, and for anyone who is starting out on a fitness programme.

Walking costs nothing and is easy to incorporate into your daily routine. In addition, it puts little strain on the joints and muscles, which makes injury less likely than in running, for example, although remember that no activity is guaranteed risk free.

Plot one or more routes that are between 1.6 and 6.5km (1 and 4 miles) long, and aim to walk 3–4 times a week, each time increasing the distance that you walk or improving your time. The effort you invest will determine how quickly your overall fitness level improves. Initially you will probably make good progress. From then on, walking more briskly, putting greater effort into your arm movements and including some gradients in your routes will all help to keep your heart at about 60–75% of your TTZ (see p. 21).

The table opposite offers both time and distance targets, although you will almost certainly find that your pace automatically increases as you exercise more. If, as a beginner, you cannot walk 3.2km (2 miles) in around 35 minutes,

don't increase your distance until you can. Once you have worked your way through the four levels of the programme, you should be able to walk 1.6km (1 mile) in 10–12 minutes. When you reach that target, you will need to walk 4.8–6.4km (3–4 miles) three times a week to maintain an adequate level of fitness.

When you walk, start slowly and take the time to mobilize your upper body. When that is moving well, work on your lower body, then stop and do some short stretches. For the major period of the walk increase your pace and stride using your arms as you walk. If you are walking with a partner, you should be able to talk to each other comfortably.

If you find that you are breathing hard or sweating heavily, or if you are monitoring your pulse rate and find that it is too high, reduce the pace until you are breathing with ease and your pulse has returned to its exercise normal. At the end of the walk, spend 5–10 minutes stretching your upper and lower body, with the emphasis on your calves, thighs and hips.

Posture and technique are important in walking. Breathe normally. Keep your back straight, chest lifted, chin up, shoulders relaxed and abdominals pulled in tightly. Bend your arms at the elbows and keep your elbows close to your body. Swing your arms from the shoulders, raising them toward your chest and back so that they are in line with your hips, but no higher. (This technique takes time to develop so keep at it.) Your feet should work from heel to toe and, as your technique improves, place more emphasis on the hip of the forward leg. Try to keep a low centre of gravity.

Wear loose, comfortable clothing (pp. 32–33) and lightweight shoes that breathe and are cushioned. Choose lightweight cotton socks.

Your aim is to complete the distances stated in the times given. Don't move on to the following week's sessions until you can do so comfortably.

Different routes mean that you won't become bored. Woodland and parks hold more interest, but walking to work is equally beneficial.

WALKING PROGRAMME

WEEK		1	2	3	4	5	6	7	8	9	10
BEG.	Per week	2	3	3	3	3	3	3	3	3	3
	Time min	20	30	40	38	36	34	45	40	38	50
	Dist. km	1.6	2.4	3.2	3.2	3.2	3.2	4	4	4	4.8
	miles	1	1½	2	2	2	2	2½	2½	2½	3
INTER.	Per week	3	3	3	3	3	3	3	3	3	3
	Time min	38	36	34	32	40	38	36	48	46	43
	Dist. km	3.2	3.2	3.2	3.2	4	4	4	4.8	4.8	4.8
	miles	2	2	2	2	2½	2½	2½	3	3	3
ADV.	Per week	3	3	3	3	3	3	3	3	3	3
	Time min	36	34	32	40	38	34	46	44	42	38
	Dist. km	3.2	3.2	3.2	4	4	4	4.8	4.8	4.8	4.8
	miles	2	2	2	2½	2½	2½	3	3	3	3
EXP.	Per week	3	4	4	4	4	4	4	4	4	4
	Time min	40	38	50	44	40	38	48	46	44	40
	Dist. km	4.8	4.8	5.6	5.6	5.6	5.6	6.4	6.4	6.4	6.4
	miles	3	3	3½	3½	3½	3½	4	4	4	4

ENDURANCE • Jogging and running

Both running and its slower form jogging are convenient, affordable, flexible, maintainable, satisfying and produce numerous psychological benefits. Anybody who is reasonably fit can run or jog: neither requires advanced booking or a special location, and both are easy to fit into your schedule. And, since jogging is now so popular, most towns and cities have running clubs, making it easy for you to find someone to run with.

Running and jogging increase strength in the legs and lead to good improvements in the cardio-vascular and respiratory systems. They also raise your metabolic rate, both while you are running and for up to eight hours afterward, which burns off calories.

There is enormous satisfaction to be derived from running. Long-distance runners experience what is commonly known as "runners' high", a euphoria thought to be caused by the stimulation of the release of endorphins, chemicals that occur naturally in the body and have a similar effect to that of morphine. Even if you don't run long enough to get "high", you will find that you have a feeling of well-being, and are better able to cope with the stresses of everyday life.

Each week complete all the sessions detailed under that week in your fitness level. If only a time is given, run for that time regardless of distance. If only a distance is given, run that far regardless of the time it takes.

JOGGING AND RUNNING PROGRAMME

WEEK		1	2	3	4	5	6	7	8	9	10
BEG.	Per week	2	3	5	5	3	3	2	5	3	3
	Time min	—	15	14	12	12	11	10	16	16	14
	Dist. km	1.6	1.6	1.6	1.6	1.6	1.6	1.6	2.4	2.4	2.4
	miles	1	1	1	1	1	1	1	1½	1½	1½
	Per week	1	2	—	—	2	2	3	—	2	2
	Time min	—	—	—	—	—	18	18	—	22	21
	Dist. km	2.4	3.2	—	—	2.4	2.4	2.4	—	3.2	3.2
	miles	1½	2	—	—	1½	1½	1½	—	2	2
INTER.	Per week	3	4	4	4	3	4	3	4	3	4
	Time min	18	18	24	23	17	22	—	22	17	21
	Dist. km	3.2	3.2	4	4	3.2	4	3.2	4	3.2	4
	miles	2	2	2½	2½	2	2½	2	2½	2	2½
	Per week	2	1	1	1	2	1	2	1	2	1
	Time min	—	—	—	40	—	50	45	60	36	65
	Dist. km	4.8	6.4	6.4	—	6.4	—	8	—	6.4	—
	miles	3	4	4	—	4	—	5	—	4	—

IDENTIFYING YOUR GOALS
The running programme here is designed eventually to take you through to a full marathon in a time of 4–5 hours. If this is not your goal, you should reach an acceptable degree of fitness by the beginning of the intermediate level. After that, run a minimum of 4.8km (3 miles) three times a week to maintain your fitness. If you cross train with other activities, you have the basis of an excellent routine.

If you continue with the running programme, by about the middle of the advanced stage you should have enough stamina to run 10km (6.2 miles) comfortably, probably in less than an hour. Make a race over this distance one of your goals. To do this, you also need to include some speed work over shorter distances in your programme.

The idea of the speed work, also known as *fartlecking*, is to work in short bursts, gradually building to

JOGGING AND RUNNING PROGRAMME

WEEK		1	2	3	4	5	6	7	8	9	10
ADV.	Per week	3	5	3	4	4	4	4	3	3	1
	Time min	—	36	26	35	25	—	—	—	24	23
	Dist. km	4.8	6.4	4.8	6.4	4.8	6.4	6.4	8	4.8	4.8
	miles	3	4	3	4	3	4	4	5	3	3
	Per week	2	—	2	1	2	1	1	2	2	4
	Time min	—	—	54	—	45	—	—	—	72	44
	Dist. km	6.4	—	9.7	12.9	8	16	12.9	12.9	12.9	8
	miles	4	—	6	8	5	10	8	8	8	5
	Per week	—	—	—	—	—	—	—	—	—	1
	Time min	—	—	—	—	—	—	—	—	—	—
	Dist. km	—	—	—	—	—	—	—	—	—	19.3
	miles	—	—	—	—	—	—	—	—	—	12
EXP.	Per week	2	2	3	4	2	1	1	3	1	2
	Time min	25	33	30	58	30	28	24	—	22	46
	Dist. km	4.8	6.4	6.4	11.3	6.4	6.4	4.8	8	4.8	9.7
	miles	3	4	4	7	4	4	3	5	3	6
	Per week	3	3	2	1	3	4	4	2	4	3
	Time min	70	—	68	—	—	50	57	65	63	—
	Dist. km	12.7	12.7	12.7	16	11.3	9.7	11.3	12.7	12.7	12.7
	miles	8	8	8	10	7	6	7	8	8	8
	Per week	—	—	—	—	—	1	—	1	—	1
	Time min	—	—	—	—	—	—	—	—	—	80
	Dist. km	—	—	—	—	—	16	—	16	—	16
	miles	—	—	—	—	—	10	—	10	—	10

ENDURANCE • Jogging and running

run more and more of the 10km (6.2 miles) as a "short burst". You don't have to sprint all your short bursts: try skipping too. The important point is to include some bursts of faster activity and some walking so that you keep working at the lower end of your TTZ (see p. 21).

You must allow sufficient rest between the sprints. These sessions train your body's anaerobic system to become more efficient (see also pp. 12–13 and 68–69). Try to time the sprints: for maximum effect, these bursts need last for only 40 seconds. As you progress, build them up to 2 to 5 minutes with

slow work in between. As you get fitter you can cut down the rest or low-level activity between bursts.

You must allow rest days or do a different activity between long runs. As your body becomes more efficient at using energy over the weeks, your ability to keep going without becoming exhausted will improve. You will also burn calories, so it is vital to eat well (see pp. 212–13) and get plenty of sleep.

Don't do too much too soon. The programme offers an indication of what you can hope to achieve but everybody is different. Be guided by how you feel: if you plan a long

You don't have to run or jog outdoors: a trampoline (*below*) is ideal indoors, since the impact is minimal. Jog for the time stated and measure your "distance" using a pedometer.

run and feel below par, take a short run instead: you are most susceptible to injury when you feel unwell.

HOW AND WHERE TO RUN

Good posture makes injury less likely. Keep upright (don't slouch) and lift your rib cage from your waist so that your diaphragm functions properly. Pull your abdominals in, relax your shoulders and keep your head high. Bend your elbows, and keep your wrists lower than your elbows with your hands relaxed and fingers curled. Your arms should be slightly away from your body and swing easily.

Run with a heel-first motion, with a clawing action as the rest of your foot hits the ground. Push off from the ball of your foot at each stride. Start with small strides, then experiment until you find a natural stride length. Keep your knees high. Breathe regularly, emphasizing the exhalation. You should be able to talk to a partner as you run. Check that you are working within your TTZ (see p. 21).

Good shoes are vital. Choose a pair with cushioned heels, stable supports to the foot and ankle and a wide midsole (see p. 35). Dress appropriately for the conditions (see p. 33) and wear bright clothing and reflector strips at night.

Don't forget to warm up and cool down, and stretch. Runners often suffer with poor hamstrings and calves so work on strengthening and stretching these areas in particular.

If your lower back and abdomen are weak, work on those too. Look at how your shoes are wearing; if you are landing more heavily on one side than the other you could be storing up problems. Inserts may correct the imbalance but it is wise to consult an osteopath.

When you begin, or when you intensify your programme, you may experience soreness or discomfort. This is your body adjusting to a new level of activity and will abate if you work out on alternate days and do plenty of stretching.

Drink as much water as you can before, during and after a run. Each hour, you are likely to sweat 1–2 litres (1¾–3½pt) of water. If you are thirsty afterward, you weren't drinking enough and may be dehydrated.

Measure your routes (have more than one for variety) using a map or pedometer, or in the car. Run on grass wherever you can. If you have to use the road, check that the surface is smooth and stable. Uneven surfaces may cause tendon and ligament problems. If you run on a graded surface, go back the way you came to balance the stress on your body. Try to choose low-traffic areas and avoid wet, slippery and icy surfaces.

Finally, a note on safety. Run where it is well lit. If you use a personal stereo, keep the volume low. Carry a personal alarm and be aware of people around you. And always tell someone where you are going and how long you will be.

ENDURANCE • Swimming

Generally regarded as the best all-round form of exercise, swimming works all the major muscle groups and has an aerobic effect. The water bears your weight and cushions impact so that there is no stress on your joints. And the risk of injury is low, which is one reason why swimming is often included in rehabilitation programmes for those who have sustained sports injuries and who have mobility problems.

Swimming is, however, the poor relation in the family of aerobic exercises. Running, cross-country skiing and cycling all use your cardiovascular system more efficiently. Nonetheless, for many people it is a gentle and accessible way of building up and maintaining heart and lung fitness, and it works more muscles than both running and cycling.

Swimming capability varies a great deal from one person to another. Swimming is a technical sport, and if your technique is not good, you may find it difficult. If you are a beginner or if you would like to improve your technique, ask whether the pool you use offers classes. Concentrate on smoothness and ease of stroke and don't force the action. Once your strokes are efficient, your swimming will

Each week complete all the sessions detailed under that week in your fitness level. If only a time is given, swim for that time no matter how many lengths you do. If only a distance is given, swim that far no matter how long it takes.

SWIMMING PROGRAMME

WEEK		1	2	3	4	5	6	7	8	9	10
BEG.	Per week	2	2	2	3	3	5	3	5	3	5
	Time min	—	—	—	—	—	14	12	16	15	20
	Dist. m	50	50	100	150	250	300	300	400	400	500
	yd	55	55	110	165	275	330	330	440	440	550
	Per week	—	2	3	3	2	—	2	—	2	—
	Time min	—	—	—	—	15	—	—	—	—	—
	Dist. m	—	100	150	200	300	—	400	—	500	—
	yd	—	110	165	220	330	—	440	—	550	—
INTER.	Per week	4	3	5	3	5	2	3	5	3	5
	Time min	5	5	8	7	10	12	11	14	13	15
	Dist. m	200	200	300	300	400	500	500	600	600	700
	yd	220	220	330	330	440	550	550	660	660	770
	Per week	—	2	—	2	—	3	2	—	2	—
	Time min	—	8	—	13	—	—	16	—	19	—
	Dist. m	—	300	—	500	—	400	700	—	800	—
	yd	—	330	—	550	—	440	770	—	880	—

improve: poor stroke technique makes workouts tiring which can affect your motivation.

As with other activities, the more efficient you become, the more you have to do to achieve results. This is not as daunting as it sounds, however, since as you start to swim more efficiently, your buoyancy and your ability to push yourself through the water also improve and you will find it easier to add on extra lengths.

YOUR SWIMMING PROGRAMME

If you are already a competent swimmer, and especially if you can swim front crawl continuously for 100m (110yd) or more, start the programme at intermediate level. The same applies if you are adept at backstroke, which is almost as fast as front crawl when swum well but which has a breathing technique that is easier to master. Its chief disadvantage is that it is difficult to see other swimmers.

SWIMMING PROGRAMME

WEEK		1	2	3	4	5	6	7	8	9	10
ADV.	Per week	2	2	2	2	2	2	2	2	2	2
	Time min	14	13	13	21	21	20	26	26	25	25
	Dist. m	500	500	500	800	800	800	1,000	1,000	1,000	1,000
	yd	550	550	550	880	880	880	1,100	1,100	1,100	1,100
	Per week	3	3	3	3	2	2	2	3	3	3
	Time min	11	10	18	17	16	21	25	32	30	32
	Dist. m	500	500	800	800	800	1,000	1,100	1,200	1,400	1,450
	yd	550	550	880	880	880	1,100	1,210	1,320	1,540	1,595
	Per week	—	—	—	—	—	1	1	—	—	—
	Time min	—	—	—	—	—	—	—	—	—	—
	Dist. m	—	—	—	—	—	1,100	1,400	—	—	—
	yd	—	—	—	—	—	1,210	1,540	—	—	—
EXP.	Per week	2	2	2	2	3	2	2	2	2	3
	Time min	12	10	12	18	20	11	18	22	23	22
	Dist. m	500	500	500	800	800	800	1,000	1,200	1,000	1,000
	yd	550	550	550	880	880	880	1,100	1,320	1,100	1,100
	Per week	3	3	3	3	2	2	2	3	3	3
	Time min	10	8	16	16	16	20	25	31	30	38
	Dist. m	500	500	800	800	800	1,000	1,100	1,400	1,400	1,800
	yd	550	550	880	880	880	1,100	1,210	1,540	1,540	1,980
	Per week	—	—	—	—	—	1	1	—	1	—
	Time min	—	—	—	—	—	—	—	—	—	—
	Dist. m	—	—	—	—	—	1,100	1,400	—	1,500	—
	yd	—	—	—	—	—	1,210	1,540	—	1,650	—

ENDURANCE • Swimming

To achieve a training effect, you have to raise your pulse rate to 120–140 beats per minute and keep it there for 20–30 minutes or more. When you swim, it is easy to slow down and swim below your TTZ (see p. 21). Swimming up and down using only one stroke may not produce the improvements you want; to continue to improve, your sessions need to be structured.

As you progress through the levels you should aim to vary the strokes you use, including more and more lengths of front crawl and backstroke. (You will probably need to do this in any case to achieve the target times.) Add in some sprint swimming (as fast as you can for a short period) and aerobic swimming (building up the length of time you spend swimming to at least 20–30 minutes, without concern for lengths) and you have the basis of an excellent endurance-building programme. A word of warning: don't do the most intense sessions in the programmes on consecutive days; work off the effects of a hard session with a gentle swim or jog. Allow rest periods and get plenty of sleep.

Whatever your level, warm up with some mobility exercises for the upper body and swim a few lengths leisurely, then start the appropriate time and distance. Keep a check on your pulse and slow down if you find that you become breathless (test yourself at the end of the pool, not in the middle of a length). Don't exceed

By the time you reach advanced level, you should be mixing your strokes. Try to spend an equal time on front crawl, backstroke, breaststroke and butterfly – if you can manage it, although butterfly is not easy.

your safe maximum. Stretch – out of the pool – after your cool down. The best strength exercise, which will improve all your strokes as well as your flexibility, is the lat pull down (p. 117). Others to include are upright rows, forward raises, bench presses, bent forward lateral raises, bent arm pullovers, barbell curls, calf raises, squats, leg extensions and hamstring curls. It is important to be equally strong in the back and front of your body.

PRACTICAL CONSIDERATIONS

The distances in the programmes are in metres (yards). Ask the pool attendant the length of the pool (if it is not already marked) to work out how many lengths you need to do: one less does make a difference so don't cheat.

Be aware of the temperature of the pool: a good working temperature is around 28°C (82°F). If the water feels cold after you have been in for some time, your muscles may tense and tighten;

water that is too warm on the other hand will make you drowsy.

Don't swim within 1–2 hours of eating. Eat carbohydrates and drink water immediately afterward. If you are swimming in your lunch break, don't skip lunch: you need to replenish your energy. Go prepared.

EXERCISES IN THE WATER

Props can help you to improve your strength and technique. A kickboard in your hands at arm's length makes you work your legs. Alternatively, hold the kickboard between your feet and use only your arms to swim with.

Some pools also offer aerobic water workouts which add variety to your programme, as well as being great fun. Check that the teacher is qualified and that the tempo of the music is not too fast otherwise you could slip and injure yourself. If you are going to do this more than once a week, it is probably worth investing in specially designed aerobic shoes.

MUSCLE GROUPS USED IN SWIMMING

Backstroke	Latissimus dorsi, teres major and minor, deltoids, pectorals, rhomboids, trapezius, biceps, brachialis.
Front crawl	Deltoids, teres major and minor, trapezius, rhomboids, latissimus dorsi, pectorals, biceps, brachialis, triceps, wrist and hand flexors, quadriceps, gluteals, hamstrings, adductors, gastrocnemius, feet flexors.
Breaststroke	Quadriceps, gluteals, hamstrings, adductors, latissimus dorsi, triceps, deltoids.
Butterfly	Quadriceps, gluteals, hamstrings, adductors, gastrocnemius, feet flexors, latissimus dorsi, rhomboids, teres major, pectorals, subscapularis, biceps, brachialis, wrist flexors.

ENDURANCE • Rowing

A rowing machine cannot duplicate the sensation of rowing on water, but it does provide a good substitute and works the same groups of muscles in the legs, buttocks, back, abdomen, shoulders and arms. Rowing is often overlooked in aerobic training, since it can be hard work.

It is worth remembering, however, that rowing provides total body exercise and is a good activity to include in a cross-training programme, alternated with running or cycling. It is also ideal if you find that impact sports cause you problems. The majority of lower back injuries in rowers are caused by poor technique, or by poor flexibility in the back.

Keep your back flat and your abdominals pulled in and aim for a smooth, steady movement. Don't rest between repetitions. If you are a beginner, adjust the resistance on the machine so that it is light enough for you to work with good technique. Be cautious until you are confident that your strokes are smooth and proficient. A sensible starting rate is around 10 strokes per minute, increasing to 12 and up as you progress. The better your aerobic fitness, the greater the stroke rate should be.

To improve your strength for rowing use squats for your legs and cleans for your whole body. Lat pull downs, barbell rows, seated rows and lower back raises will strengthen your back; you should also work on your biceps and your abdominals.

ANAEROBIC TRAINING

The programme here is designed primarily to improve your aerobic fitness and your overall muscle tone. At the end of the beginners' programme, when you are completing 20 minutes work, start to increase the intensity of the

ROWING PROGRAMME										
WEEK	1	2	3	4	5	6	7	8	9	10
BEG. Per week	1	1	1	1	1	1	1	3	1	1
Time min	5	6	8	9	·11	13	15	17	17	19
Per week	—	2	2	2	2	2	2	—	2	2
Time min	—	7	9	10	12	14	16	—	18	20
INTER. Per week	1	1	1	1	3	1	1	1	1	1
Time min	14	15	16	17	18	19	21	22	23	25
Per week	2	3	2	2	—	1	2	2	1	2
Time min	15	16	17	18	—	20	22	23	24	26
Per week	—	—	—	—	—	1	—	—	2	—
Time min	—	—	—	—	—	21	—	—	25	—

workout by adding short bursts of explosive activity, working harder and faster, increasing the stroke rate and/or resistance. If you are using a machine in a gym it may include a computerized programme that sets these bursts for you.

These intense bursts work your anaerobic system (see pp. 12–13). The anaerobic threshold – the point at which lactic acid builds up faster than your body can remove it – varies from person to person; assessing where yours is can be tricky. The signs that you have reached it are rapid breathing (your body is trying to get more oxygen into the system) and a burning sensation or cramp in your muscles. This type of training is the only way to increase your tolerance to lactic acid and, therefore, your ability to exercise without muscle fatigue.

Warm up and do some short stretches before starting the major work of the session. Row for the times indicated, each week completing all the sessions detailed under that week in your fitness level. Don't do the longer sessions on consecutive days. Cool down and stretch at the end.

ROWING PROGRAMME											
WEEK		1	2	3	4	5	6	7	8	9	10
ADV.	Per week	2	1	2	4	3	1	1	4	3	1
	Time min	23	24	26	27	28	29	30	32	33	34
	Per week	2	3	3	1	2	4	3	1	2	4
	Time min	24	25	27	28	29	30	31	33	34	35
EXP.	Per week	1	3	1	3	2	4	3	5	3	2
	Time min	31	32	33	32	34	35	36	38	39	43
	Per week	3	2	4	2	3	1	2	—	1	3
	Time min	32	33	32	33	35	36	37	—	40	45
	Per week	—	—	—	—	—	—	—	—	1	—
	Time min	—	—	—	—	—	—	—	—	42	—

ENDURANCE • Cycling

Cycling builds your leg muscles and is an effective means of working your cardiovascular system. And, since these large muscles generate great quantities of lactic acid, thereby increasing your tolerance to its build-up, cycling is also good anaerobic exercise.

One of its drawbacks is that it does not involve carrying your whole body weight, but this is offset by its low impact on the joints. Nor does it work your upper body. Probably its biggest drawback, however, is cost: a good-quality bicycle (even secondhand) can be expensive. Are you sure you want cycling to be the major component of your fitness programme?

When you ride a good-quality bicycle, most of your effort is used against air resistance or drag, not in forward propulsion. Since drag increases in proportion to relative wind speed, an increase in wind or cycling speed creates extra resistance. Gradient also affects the amount of work you have to do. If you are a beginner, work hard enough to sweat a little and keep within your TTZ (see p. 21).

Leg extensions are good for cyclists, along with hamstring curls, bench presses, lower back raises, squats, calf raises and crunches.

It is difficult to be accurate about target times and distances when cycling outdoors since wind speed and gradients play such a large part. Concentrate on time, each week completing all the sessions detailed for your fitness level.

CYCLING PROGRAMME										
WEEK	1	2	3	4	5	6	7	8	9	10
BEG. Per week	3	3	3	3	3	3	3	3	3	3
Time min	10	12	11	17	10	16	15	14	13	18
Dist. km	—	3.2	3.2	4.8	3.2	4.8	4.8	4.8	4.8	6.4
miles	—	2	2	3	2	3	3	3	3	4
Per week	—	2	2	2	2	2	2	2	2	2
Time min	—	15	18	25	30	35	38	40	42	45
Dist. km	—	—	4.8	—	8	—	9.7	—	11.3	—
miles	—	—	3	—	5	—	6	—	7	—
INTER. Per week	3	3	3	3	3	3	3	4	3	4
Time min	20	16	20	24	15	28	18	26	14	22
Dist. km	8	6.4	8	9.7	6.4	11.3	8	11.3	6.4	9.7
miles	5	4	5	6	4	7	5	7	4	6
Per week	2	2	2	2	2	2	2	1	2	1
Time min	55	40	50	—	48	58	45	—	53	—
Dist. km	16	12.9	16	19.3	16	19.3	16	24	19.3	32
miles	10	8	10	12	10	12	10	15	12	20

Beginners often start in too high a gear. Concentrate on increasing your pedalling speed. Also, vary the terrain to include some hills. At intermediate level, add short (½–1min) bursts of speed work twice in each 20–30 minute session, once near the middle and once toward the end. At advanced level, increase this to four or five bursts of 2–2½ minutes each. Experts aim for ten 1.6km (1 mile) intervals with ½–1 minute rests between.

CYCLING PROGRAMME											
WEEK		1	2	3	4	5	6	7	8	9	10
ADV.	Per week	3	3	3	2	2	3	2	4	2	2
	Time min	21	25	30	17	13	19	22	26	25	32
	Dist. km	9.7	11.3	12.9	8	6.4	9.7	11.3	12.9	6.4	16
	miles	6	7	8	5	4	6	7	8	4	10
	Per week	2	2	2	3	2	2	2	1	2	2
	Time min	50	—	—	40	58	—	54	—	52	70
	Dist. km	19.3	19.3	32	16	24	24	24	24	24	32
	miles	12	12	20	10	15	15	15	15	15	20
	Per week	—	—	—	—	1	—	1	—	1	1
	Time min	—	—	—	—	—	—	115	—	—	110
	Dist. km	—	—	—	—	48	—	48	—	48	48
	miles	—	—	—	—	30	—	30	—	30	30
EXP.	Per week	3	3	3	3	4	3	2	4	2	2
	Time min	25	28	17	22	25	22	30	30	32	40
	Dist. km	11.3	12.9	8	11.3	12.9	12.9	14.4	14.4	16	19.3
	miles	7	8	5	7	8	8	9	9	10	12
	Per week	2	2	2	2	2	2	2	1	2	2
	Time min	55	67	40	54	65	65	62	—	60	85
	Dist. km	19.3	32	16	24	32	32	32	40	32	40
	miles	12	20	10	15	20	20	20	25	20	25
	Per week	—	—	—	1	1	—	1	—	1	1
	Time min	—	—	—	115	—	—	105	—	—	120
	Dist. km	—	—	—	48	56	—	48	—	64	64
	miles	—	—	—	30	35	—	30	—	40	40

ENDURANCE • Skipping

An excellent and often neglected way to work your aerobic system and improve your aerobic endurance, skipping is a low-impact exercise and a good calorie burner. Skipping also gives your calves, thighs and buttocks a good workout without putting your knees under stress (since your feet should stay in close contact with the ground). In addition, it works your back and shoulders and helps to improve the range of movement in your shoulder joints.

There are scores of skipping ropes on the market, many of which are only suitable as children's toys. For fitness skipping, you need one that is hard wearing, so choose polyurethane, plastic or rubber. Some models have swivel handles, which make the action smoother. The correct length is also important: stand with both feet on the centre of the rope. The handles should reach under your armpits; a rope that is any longer or shorter will make your workout difficult.

Skipping always looks easier than it is but can quickly become exhausting. If you haven't touched a rope since you were a child, skip for a couple of minutes (time it). If you find this too difficult, do 30–40 skips, then rest for 30 seconds. Repeat twice more.

At your next session do the same, but reduce the rest periods by 5 seconds. Continue in this way until you have eliminated the rest periods completely. You are now ready to start the beginners' programme.

Start with a "rocking" skip, stepping with the same foot leading. Then try alternating your leading foot. Always keep your feet within 2.5cm (1in) of the ground and your knees slightly bent to absorb impact. As you get more efficient, jump with both feet together and try one foot hops and other variations. (There are now videos available on skipping which will give you some ideas if you find it difficult to come up with variations.)

		1	2	3	4	5	6	7	8	9	10
WEEK		1	2	3	4	5	6	7	8	9	10
BEG.	Per week	1	2	2	3	3	2	2	3	3	3
	Time min	3	4	5	7	8	9	11	14	17	20
	Per week	—	—	—	—	—	1	—	—	—	—
	Time min	—	—	—	—	—	10	—	—	—	—
INTER.	Per week	2	3	3	3	3	2	1	3	3	3
	Time min	5	6	7	8	10	12	14	20	22	25
	Per week	—	—	—	—	—	1	—	—	—	—
	Time min	—	—	—	—	—	13	—	—	—	—

SKIPPING PROGRAMME

Keep your shoulders relaxed with your upper arms close to your body. Use your wrists – which should be at hip height – to turn the rope. Make sure that your back is straight and your abdominals are pulled in. Keep your head up and in line with your spine.

Skipping can be great fun and it is always worth taking a rope out for interval training when you run (see p. 62), or including it in your circuit training. It is also beneficial if you play basketball, volleyball, hockey and most racket sports since it develops your coordination and agility.

Wear loose, comfortable clothing to skip. The best shoes are aerobics shoes which offer the stability your feet need. Since skipping is a low-impact activity, surfaces are not really a problem but try to avoid uneven ground.

SKIPPING PROGRAMME											
WEEK		1	2	3	4	5	6	7	8	9	10
ADV.	Per week	3	3	3	3	3	2	1	3	4	4
	Time min	8	10	12	14	16	18	20	26	29	32
	Per week	—	—	—	—	—	1	—	—	—	—
	Time min	—	—	—	—	—	19	—	—	—	—
EXP.	Per week	3	3	3	3	4	3	2	4	5	5
	Time min	12	14	16	18	21	24	27	33	36	40
	Per week	—	—	—	—	—	1	—	—	—	—
	Time min	—	—	—	—	—	26	—	—	—	—

STRENGTH • Introduction

Muscular strength is the ability of a muscle or a group of muscles to exert maximum force to overcome a resistance. That resistance is usually provided by weights, either free (as in a barbell, *below*, or set of dumbbells) or fixed to a stack on the end of a lever or cable.

As you weight train, your muscles become stronger as you increase the weights you are using. "Pure" strength, however, is not what most people want, after a certain level at least. Then, tone becomes important. For this you reduce the weight you are lifting but lift it many more times. This is usually referred to as muscular endurance: the ability of a muscle or group of muscles to exert force to overcome resistance continuously for extended periods of time.

WHY STRENGTH TRAIN?

Aside from the importance of muscular strength for sports players and for overall fitness (see also pp. 10–11), the main reason for embarking on a strength-training programme is that this is the most effective way to change your body's physical appearance and the only means of changing the size and density of your muscles. A lean, well-proportioned body only comes from losing body fat and gaining muscle.

A note for women: do not feel that working with weights will give you a body builder's figure – it won't. Women have a different proportion of testosterone (the muscle-stimulating hormone) from men and it is this that allows men's muscles to bulk up. Women body builders achieve their physique by training 2–4 hours a day with extremely heavy weights. Training will give you strong muscles but not the same bulk as those of a man.

WHEN TO TRAIN

Train at a regular time so that you are physically and mentally prepared for the work. Experiment to find the time that "works" for you.

Leave at least 24 hours between weight-training sessions. If you don't want to be idle, choose an activity that allows your muscles to

recuperate. If your muscles are still sore at the next workout, your rest period wasn't long enough.

SETS AND REPS

A rep (repetition) is one execution of an exercise. A set is a series of repetitions worked with little or no pause between them.

For a muscle to increase in size, it must be taxed to the full, which usually means 6–12 repetitions. After that, it will not increase in strength, but in endurance. For strength, you also usually need to work 3–6 sets (1–2 for beginners).

If you are working to gain strength using heavy weights, rest for a couple of minutes between sets. When you are working with light weights and many repetitions, rest for less than a minute between sets. Work as hard as you can in each set, with good technique for every repetition. Most of the exercises here take 4–6 seconds per rep to work properly.

The most common cause of poor technique is working with weights that are too heavy before you are ready. Always start with light weights. A weight that allows you to work all but the last two reps comfortably is about right: the last two should always be a challenge.

ABOUT THE EXERCISES

In exercises that involve working your left then your right side, work the sets and reps indicated for *each* side. All the exercises tell you when to breathe in and out. Usually you exhale as you exert maximum force but check the instructions carefully.

It is advisable to work with a partner, particularly if you are using heavy weights. This is essential if you are exercising lying on a bench that doesn't have a rack (it is advisable even if your bench does have a rack). Make sure that any partner can do the exercise you are working correctly and is strong enough to take a weight from you. Do not partner anyone yourself unless you can do both.

AT THE GYM

Many of the free weight exercises here can be worked using machines in the gym, if you prefer. Be aware, however, that many machines are designed for those over 1.67m (5ft 7in); if you are shorter, you may have problems "fitting" the equipment. Adjustable machines are more common these days but check before you use a machine. A machine that is the wrong size for your body at best is a waste of effort, at worst could lead to injury.

The position of the weight stack in relation to the machine alters the force you must exert to move the stack. For this reason don't take your free weight load as the figure to use on a machine (and vice versa). Start again with a low minimum and increase it until you are happy. And always check that the pin is secure in the weight stack (ask an attendant if you have any doubts).

STRENGTH • Standing and lifting

THE DEAD LIFT Areas worked: Front of thighs, buttocks, back of thighs, lower back
Muscles used: Quadriceps, gluteals, hamstrings, erector spinae

PHASE 1
1 Stand centred on a barbell with your feet slightly more than hip width apart, knees in line with your toes and your toes facing forward under the bar.

2 Keep your back straight, chest lifted and abdominals in. Tilt your pelvis forward.

3 Keep your hips square. Bend at the hips and knees. Place your forearms on your knees.

PHASE 2
4 Lean forward slightly so that your shoulders are forward of your knees and the bar. Raise your buttocks so that they are higher than your knees, but not as high as your shoulders.

5 Keep your head in line with your spine and look down slightly.

6 With your hands wider than your feet, take an overhand grip on the bar. Take a deep breath in.

PHASE 3
7 Breathe out as you straighten your legs to stand up, pressing from your heels. Work slowly: lead with your shoulders and use your legs, not the back of your arms, to lift. Keep both feet on the floor.

8 Keeping your arms straight and the bar close to your body, raise the bar to your thighs. Keep your abdominals tight; don't overextend your knees.

9 To lower the barbell, breathe in as you bend your knees. Keep your back flat and the bar close to your body.

Note: To lift dumbbells, place the weights outside and at right angles to your feet, then lift as a barbell.

AVOIDING PROBLEMS
Simple precautions in your everyday life can prevent problems later.
• If you sit at a desk all day, try not to round your shoulders. This can cause back and neck injuries.
• Displaced weight tilts the spine and can affect your hip alignment. Two avoidable causes of badly aligned hips are carrying a heavy bag on the same shoulder and carrying a child on the same hip. Change sides regularly.
• Wearing high heels, or leaving shoes unlaced over a period of months can lead to back problems.
• Sit on a chair or sofa for a long time before buying. Check that the height and depth of the seat fit your body.

HOW TO GRIP

1 Use an overhand grip with your thumb under the weight and knuckles up.

2 Keep your wrist straight and locked. Since wrists tend to be weak (especially in women), you may need to do extra work on them to lift heavy weights.

Note: Keeping your wrist straight avoids strain or injury. It also ensures the correct technique in exercises such as shoulder and bench presses (pp. 107, 124–25) and upright rows (p. 110). Only to work flies (p. 127) do slightly bent wrists avoid strain.

BELTS AND SUPPORTS

Belts, wraps and other supports allow the major muscles being worked to be used to their greatest extent, without being limited by weaker muscles. Belts work by contracting the muscles surrounding the spine, abdomen and rib cage, thereby increasing the pressure within the abdomen and stabilizing the spine. The abdomen acts as a strong, rigid lever which can exert great force when you are lifting. Belts are not necessary in weight training since you should be working toward a well-balanced body with no areas weaker than others. They do have their uses in weightlifting, however, and if you are doing exercises such as squats using heavy weights.

If you do use a belt, wear it as tight as you can, but leave enough room to take a deep breath. If you are buying a belt, choose a model that is no more than 10cm (4in) wide: anything wider could interfere with your technique.

HOW TO STAND

Stand with your feet slightly more than hip width apart, toes forward and body weight on the balls of your feet. Bend your knees slightly. You will be able to feel your hips tilt forward. Keep your chest lifted, abdominals in and head in line with your spine.

Poor posture (*right*) is harmful. Take a look in the mirror. Does your neck strain forward with your chin toward your chest? (Keep it level.) Do you have round shoulders? (Roll them back and down to relax them.) Does your stomach protrude?

STRENGTH • Legs

BEGINNERS' & INTERMEDIATE LUNGES

Areas worked: Thighs, buttocks
Muscles used: Quadriceps, hamstrings, gluteals

PHASE 1

1 Stand with your back straight, chest lifted and abdominals in. Tilt your pelvis forward.

2 Place your feet hip width apart with your toes pointing forward. Bend your knees slightly. Keep your hips square to the front and knees in line with your feet.

PHASE 2

3 Breathe in as you take a comfortable step forward with your right foot. Keep your foot in line with your hip.

> **SAFETY TIP**
>
> Check the alignment of your leading leg – there should be a straight line through your heel, ankle, thigh and hip, so that you do not put your knee or lower back under stress.

Note: Keep your body weight centred over your hips throughout.

4 Check that your feet are still facing forward and that your right knee is positioned on the midline between your toe and heel.

5 Lower your left knee toward the floor. Beginners should stop about 15cm (6in) from the floor; intermediates aim to get a little closer (*left*).

6 Breathe out as you draw your right leg back and stand upright. Push from your heel.

7 Complete a set, then repeat stepping forward with your left leg.

	MEN					WOMEN				
WEEKS	1–2	3–4	5–6	7–8	9–10	1–2	3–4	5–6	7–8	9–10
BEG.	8x1	12x1	8x2	12x2	10x3	8x1	12x1	8x2	12x2	10x3
INTER.	8x2	12x2	8x3	12x3	16x2	8x2	12x2	8x3	12x3	16x2
ADV.	8x3	12x3	8x4	12x4	16x3	8x3	12x3	8x4	12x4	16x3
EXP.	8x4	12x4	8x4	12x4	10x5	8x4	12x4	8x4	12x4	16x4

ADVANCED LUNGES
Areas worked: Front and back of thighs, buttocks
Muscles used: Quadriceps, hamstrings, gluteals

PHASE ❶
1 Dead lift a set of dumbbells to your sides (see p. 76). Keep the weights close to your body throughout.

2 Stand as described for phase 1 of the beginners' lunge opposite.

3 Pull your shoulders back.

PHASE ❷
4 Breathe in as you take a large step forward with your right foot. Check that your feet are facing forward and that your right knee is positioned on the midline of your toe and heel.

5 Lower your left knee to 5cm (2in) from the floor.

6 Breathe out as you draw your right leg back and stand upright. Push from your heel.

7 Complete a set, then repeat stepping forward with your left leg.

EXPERT LUNGES
Areas worked: Front and back of thighs, buttocks
Muscles used: Quadriceps, hamstrings, gluteals

PHASE ❶
1 Dead lift a barbell to the front of your thighs (see p. 76).

2 Stand as described for phase 1 of the beginners' lunge.

3 Clean the bar to the receive position (see pp. 120–21).

4 Bend your knees and press the bar above your head, then lower it to your shoulders. Widen your grip.

PHASE ❷
5 Follow the directions for phase 2 of the advanced lunge above, but aim to brush the floor with your knee.

Keep your feet hip width apart

6 Breathe out as you draw your right leg back and stand upright. Push from your heel.

7 Complete a set, then repeat using your left leg.

8 When you have completed all your sets, narrow your hand grip, bend your knees, raise the bar into the receive position, then lower it to the floor (see p. 76).

STRENGTH • Legs

BEGINNERS' SQUATS Areas worked: Front and back of thighs, buttocks
Muscles used: Quadriceps, hamstrings, gluteals

PHASE 1

1 Stand with your back straight, chest lifted and abdominals in. Tilt your pelvis forward.

2 Place your feet more than hip width apart with your toes pointing forward. Bend your knees slightly. Keep your hips square to the front and knees in line with your feet.

3 Rest your hands either on the front of your thighs or on your hips. Keep your heels on the floor throughout.

PHASE 2

4 Breathe in as you bend at your knees and hips and slowly squat down. Keep your weight over your ankles.

5 Keep your back flat and chest lifted. Look forward.

6 Check that your knees are in line with your feet.

7 Don't allow the squat to go beyond seat height: keep your thighs parallel to the floor.

8 Keep your shoulders forward of the line of your mid-thigh.

9 Breathe out as you slowly stand up: lead with your shoulders and keep your back flat and heels on the floor.

PERSONAL TRAINER'S TIP

Work in front of a mirror to check that your body is aligned correctly, with your shoulders forward of your mid-thighs and your knees in line with your feet.

INTERMEDIATE SQUATS
Areas worked: Front and back of thighs, buttocks
Muscles used: Quadriceps, hamstrings, gluteals

PHASE ■
1 Follow the directions for phase 1 of the beginners' squat opposite.

Keep your back flat throughout _____

PHASE ■
2 Breathe in as you bend from your knees and hips and slowly squat down. Keep your weight over your ankles.

3 Look forward. As you squat, extend your arms straight forward at or below shoulder height.

4 Keep your back flat, chest lifted and knees in line with your feet.

5 Don't allow the squat to go beyond seat height: keep your thighs parallel to the floor.

6 Breathe out as you slowly stand up: lead with your shoulders and keep your back flat and heels on the floor.

	MEN					WOMEN				
WEEKS	1–2	3–4	5–6	7–8	9–10	1–2	3–4	5–6	7–8	9–10
BEG.	8x1	12x1	8x2	12x2	10x3	8x1	12x1	8x2	12x2	10x3
INTER.	8x2	12x2	8x3	12x3	16x2	8x2	12x2	8x3	12x3	16x2
ADV.	8x3	12x3	8x4	12x4	16x3	8x3	12x3	8x4	12x4	16x3
EXP.	8x4	12x4	8x4	12x4	10x5	8x4	12x4	8x4	12x4	16x4

STRENGTH • Legs

ADVANCED SQUATS
Areas worked: Front and back of thighs, buttocks
Muscles used: Quadriceps, hamstrings, gluteals

PHASE ▮

1 Dead lift a set of dumbbells to your sides (see p. 76).

2 Stand with your back straight, chest lifted and abdominals in. Tilt your pelvis forward.

3 Place your feet more than hip width apart with your toes pointing forward. Bend your knees slightly. Keep your hips square to the front and knees in line with your feet.

4 Make sure that your heels stay on the floor; if this is difficult, put weights under your heels.

5 Look forward. Raise the dumbbells to your shoulders. Keep your elbows bent and facing forward.

PERSONAL TRAINER'S TIP

You may find this exercise easier if you hold the weights at waist height at your sides. Keep the dumbbells close to your body.

PHASE ▮

6 Breathe in as you bend at the knees and hips and slowly squat down. Keep your weight over your ankles.

7 Keep your back flat, chest lifted and knees in line with your feet.

8 Don't allow the squat to go beyond seat height: aim to keep your thighs parallel to the floor.

9 Breathe out as you slowly stand up: lead with your shoulders and keep your back flat and heels on the floor.

10 When you have completed all your sets, lower the dumbbells to the floor (see p. 76).

EXPERT SQUATS **Areas worked:** Front and back of thighs, buttocks
Muscles used: Quadriceps, hamstrings, gluteals

PHASE 1

1 Dead lift a barbell to the front of your thighs (see p. 76).

2 Stand with your back straight, chest lifted and abdominals in. Tilt your pelvis forward.

3 Place your feet more than hip width apart with your toes pointing forward. Bend your knees slightly. Keep your hips square to the front and knees in line with your feet.

4 Clean the bar to the receive position (see pp. 120–21). Widen your grip, bend your knees and push the bar above your head, then lower it to your shoulders.

Keep your knuckles pointing up and your elbows down

PHASE 2

5 Breathe in as you bend at your knees and hips and slowly squat down. Keep your weight over your ankles.

6 Keep your back flat and chest lifted. Look forward.

7 Check that your knees are in line with your feet.

8 Don't allow the squat to go beyond seat height: keep your thighs parallel to the floor.

9 Breathe out as you slowly stand up: lead with your shoulders and keep your back flat and heels on the floor.

10 When you have completed all your sets, narrow your hand grip and lower the barbell to the floor (see p. 76).

WEEKS	MEN					WOMEN				
	1–2	3–4	5–6	7–8	9–10	1–2	3–4	5–6	7–8	9–10
BEG.	8x1	12x1	8x2	12x2	10x3	8x1	12x1	8x2	12x2	10x3
INTER.	8x2	12x2	8x3	12x3	16x2	8x2	12x2	8x3	12x3	16x2
ADV.	8x3	12x3	8x4	12x4	16x3	8x3	12x3	8x4	12x4	16x3
EXP.	8x4	12x4	8x4	12x4	10x5	8x4	12x4	8x4	12x4	16x4

STRENGTH • Legs

INTERMEDIATE PLIE SQUATS
Areas worked: Front and back of thighs, buttocks
Muscles used: Quadriceps, hamstrings, buttocks

PHASE 1
1 Dead lift a dumbbell (see p. 76) and hold it at the centre of your body with your palms facing your body.

2 Stand with your back straight, chest lifted and abdominals in. Tilt your pelvis forward.

3 Keep your hips square to the front and place your feet more than shoulder width apart. Turn your toes out at 45°.

PHASE 2
4 Relax your shoulders and look forward, then breathe in as you slowly bend at your knees and hips and squat down. Keep the dumbbell close to your body.

5 Don't allow the squat to go beyond seat height.

6 Breathe out as you slowly stand up: lead with your shoulders and keep your back flat and heels on the floor.

7 Pause briefly between repetitions. When you have completed all your sets, narrow your stance and lower the dumbbell to the floor (see p. 76).

Keep your knees in line with your feet

PERSONAL TRAINER'S TIP

This exercise is suitable for beginners if you don't use the dumbbell. Either place your hands on your hips, or rest them on the back of a chair for support.

ADVANCED & EXPERT PLIE SQUATS

Areas worked: Front and back of thighs, buttocks
Muscles used: Quadriceps, hamstrings, gluteals

1 Dead lift a set of dumbbells appropriate to your level to your sides (see p. 76). Keep your arms straight.

2 Stand with your back straight, chest lifted and abdominals in. Tilt your pelvis forward and keep your hips square to the front.

3 Place your feet more than shoulder width apart. Turn your toes out at 45°.

4 Place the dumbbells on your shoulders, with your elbows pointing out to the sides. Look forward.

5 Breathe in as you slowly bend at your knees and hips and squat down. Don't allow the squat to go beyond seat height.

6 Breathe out as you slowly stand up: lead with your shoulders and keep your back flat and heels on the floor.

7 Pause briefly between repetitions. When you have completed all your sets, narrow your stance and lower the dumbbells to the floor (see p. 76).

SQUATS TO AVOID

X Taking a squat beyond seat height opens the hinge joint of the knee to its greatest extent and puts the muscles and tendons – which control the movement – under severe stress. This is compounded if you are using weights.

WEEKS	MEN					WOMEN				
	1–2	3–4	5–6	7–8	9–10	1–2	3–4	5–6	7–8	9–10
BEG.	8x1	12x1	8x2	12x2	10x3	8x1	12x1	8x2	12x2	10x3
INTER.	8x2	12x2	8x3	12x3	16x2	8x2	12x2	8x3	12x3	16x2
ADV.	8x3	12x3	8x4	12x4	16x3	8x3	12x3	8x4	12x4	16x3
EXP.	8x4	12x4	8x4	12x4	10x5	8x4	12x4	8x4	12x4	16x4

STRENGTH • Legs

BEGINNERS' LEG EXTENSIONS Areas worked: Thighs Muscles used: Quadriceps, hamstrings

PHASE 1

1 Lie on your back and press your lower back into the floor.

2 Pull your abdominals in. Relax your head and look up.

3 Put your arms at your sides, palms flat on the floor.

4 Draw both knees toward your chest.

> **PERSONAL TRAINER'S TIP**
>
> It can be difficult to keep your lower back on the floor. A cushion either under your head or under your buttocks may help to keep your back down.

Keep your upper body relaxed and back flat on the floor

PHASE 2

5 Breathe normally as you slowly raise your lower legs toward the ceiling. Lead with your heels and keep your feet flexed and knees parallel to each other.

6 Hold briefly, keeping your knees slightly bent.

7 Breathe slowly as you lower your lower legs.

WEEKS	MEN					WOMEN				
	1–2	3–4	5–6	7–8	9–10	1–2	3–4	5–6	7–8	9–10
BEG.	8x1	12x1	8x2	12x2	10x3	8x1	12x1	8x2	12x2	10x3
INTER.	8x2	12x2	8x3	12x3	16x2	8x2	12x2	8x3	12x3	16x2
ADV.	8x3	12x3	8x4	12x4	16x3	8x3	12x3	8x4	12x4	16x3
EXP.	8x4	12x4	8x4	12x4	10x5	8x4	12x4	8x4	12x4	16x4

INTERMEDIATE LEG EXTENSIONS Areas worked: Thighs   Muscles used: Quadriceps, hamstrings

PHASE **1**
1 Lie back and prop your body on your elbows. Keep your forearms flat on the floor.

2 Keep your back flat, chest lifted and abdominals in. Look forward.

3 Keep your feet hip width apart and knees bent at 90°. Place your left foot flat on the floor, flex your right foot and breathe in.

PHASE **2**
4 Breathe out as you raise your right leg. Lead with your toes and keep your knees parallel to each other.

5 Hold briefly, without locking your knee.

6 Breathe in as you lower your leg, leading with your heel. Stop about 5cm (2in) from the floor. Hold briefly.

7 Complete a set, then repeat using your left leg.

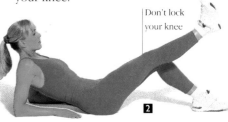

Don't lock your knee

ADVANCED & EXPERT LEG EXTENSIONS Areas worked: Front of thighs
Muscles used: Quadriceps

1 Fasten securely ankle weights appropriate to your level.

2 Sit with your back straight and the back of your knees against the edge of a bench, hip width apart.

3 Keep your chest lifted and abdominals in. Look forward.

4 Put your hands on the sides of the bench close to your body. Breathe in.

5 Breathe out as you raise your right leg. Lead with your toes and keep your foot flexed and knees parallel to each other.

6 Hold briefly, then breathe out as you lower your leg, leading with your heel. Stop about 5cm (2in) from the floor. Hold briefly.

7 Complete a set, then repeat using your left leg.

STRENGTH • Legs

MACHINE LEG EXTENSIONS Areas worked: Front and back of thighs
Muscles used: Quadriceps, hamstrings

PHASE ❶
1 Check the pin in the stack and the height and depth of the seat (see p. 75).

2 Sit with your back flat and lean back slightly. Keep your chest lifted and abdominals in. Look forward.

3 Make sure that the back of your knees are against the edge of the bench, hip width apart. Place your feet under the roller pad.

4 Keep your head in line with your spine. Place your hands on the sides of the machine close to your body.

5 Flex your feet and turn your toes toward your body.

6 Keep your knees parallel to each other and check that your ankle, knee and hip joints are all in alignment. Breathe in.

❶

PHASE ❷
7 Breathe out as you slowly raise your lower legs. Keep your knees parallel to each other.

8 Hold briefly, then breathe in as you lower your legs: lead with your heels.

❷

PERSONAL TRAINER'S TIP

This exercise is good if you play tennis or squash since it develops the muscles around the knee.

	MEN					WOMEN				
WEEKS	1–2	3–4	5–6	7–8	9–10	1–2	3–4	5–6	7–8	9–10
BEG.	8x1	12x1	8x2	12x2	10x3	8x1	12x1	8x2	12x2	10x3
INTER.	8x2	12x2	8x3	12x3	16x2	8x2	12x2	8x3	12x3	16x2
ADV.	8x3	12x3	8x4	12x4	16x3	8x3	12x3	8x4	12x4	16x3
EXP.	8x4	12x4	8x4	12x4	10x5	8x4	12x4	8x4	12x4	16x4

BEGINNERS' HAMSTRING CURLS
Areas worked: Back of thighs, buttocks
Muscles used: Hamstrings, gluteus maximus

PHASE 1
1 Lie face down on the floor.

2 Rest your head on your right forearm and extend your left arm out in front of you. Pull your abdominals in.

3 Press your hips into the floor. Keep your knees parallel to each other and flex your right foot.

4 Leading with your heel, raise your right leg off the floor. Stop with your knee about 5cm (2in) from the floor. Breathe in.

1

PHASE 2
5 Breathe out as you slowly curl your right foot toward your buttocks, leading with your heel. Keep your hips on the floor.

6 Hold briefly, then breathe in as you slowly and under control lower your leg to 5cm (2in) from the floor.

7 Complete a set, then repeat raising your left leg, with your right leg straight on the floor.

2

Keep your working knee off the floor to be sure you are working your hamstrings

WEEKS	MEN					WOMEN				
	1-2	3-4	5-6	7-8	9-10	1-2	3-4	5-6	7-8	9-10
BEG.	8x1	12x1	8x2	12x2	10x3	8x1	12x1	8x2	12x2	10x3
INTER.	8x2	12x2	8x3	12x3	16x2	8x2	12x2	8x3	12x3	16x2
ADV.	8x3	12x3	8x4	12x4	16x3	8x3	12x3	8x4	12x4	16x3
EXP.	8x4	12x4	8x4	12x4	10x5	8x4	12x4	8x4	12x4	16x4

SAFETY TIP
To avoid pulling on the ligaments and tendons of the knee, keep your knees close together.

STRENGTH • Legs

INTERMEDIATE HAMSTRING CURLS
Areas worked: Back of thighs, buttocks
Muscles used: Hamstrings, gluteus maximus

PHASE 1
1 Kneel on all fours with your knees slightly more than hip width apart.

2 Keep your back flat, head in line with your spine, arms directly beneath your shoulders and hands flat on the floor. Pull your abdominals in.

3 Breathe in as you extend your right leg so that it is parallel to the floor. Flex your foot and keep your hips square to the floor.

PHASE 2
4 Breathe out as you curl your right foot toward your buttocks.

5 Hold briefly, then breathe in as you straighten your leg. Keep your foot flexed.

6 Complete a set, then repeat using your left leg.

> ### SAFETY TIP
> If you have difficulty maintaining this body position, work hamstring curls as shown below, without weights.

ADVANCED & EXPERT HAMSTRING CURLS
Areas worked: Back of thighs, buttocks
Muscles used: Hamstrings, gluteus maximus

1 Fasten securely ankle weights appropriate to your level.

2 Stand facing, and about 60cm (2ft) away from, a wall with your hips square to the front.

3 Keep your back straight, chest lifted and abdominals in. Look forward.

4 Keep your feet hip width apart, tilt your pelvis forward and bend your knees slightly. Breathe in.

5 Breathe out as you slowly curl your right foot toward your buttocks, leading with your heel.

6 Hold briefly, then breathe in as you lower your foot to the floor. Keep your foot flexed.

7 Complete a set, then repeat using your left leg.

Keep your left leg slightly bent and knees parallel to each other

MACHINE HAMSTRING CURLS

Areas worked: Back of thighs, buttocks
Muscles used: Hamstrings, gluteus maximus

PERSONAL TRAINER'S TIP

Aim for equal strength in both legs. Initially, however, it may be easier to raise one leg at a time.

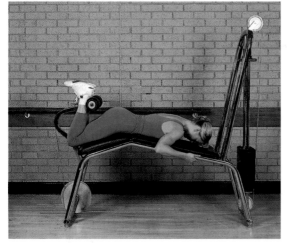

PHASE 1

1 Check the pin in the stack. Lie face down with your heels under the roller pad and knees hip width apart over the edge of the bench. Pull your abdominals in.

2 Press your hips into the bench and keep your head in line with

your spine. Rest your forehead on the bench.

3 Place your hands on the sides of the bench or out in front of you, whichever will keep your hips down and upper body in its natural S curve.

4 Flex your feet so that your toes are facing the floor. Breathe in.

PHASE 2

5 Breathe out as you bend your knees and curl your feet toward your buttocks. Lead with your heels and keep your hips firmly on the bench.

6 Hold briefly, then breathe in as you lower your legs. Don't let the weight touch the stack.

WEEKS	MEN					WOMEN				
	1–2	3–4	5–6	7–8	9–10	1–2	3–4	5–6	7–8	9–10
BEG.	8x1	12x1	8x2	12x2	10x3	8x1	12x1	8x2	12x2	10x3
INTER.	8x2	12x2	8x3	12x3	16x2	8x2	12x2	8x3	12x3	16x2
ADV.	8x3	12x3	8x4	12x4	16x3	8x3	12x3	8x4	12x4	16x3
EXP.	8x4	12x4	8x4	12x4	10x5	8x4	12x4	8x4	12x4	16x4

STRENGTH • Legs

BEGINNERS' INNER THIGH RAISES

Areas worked: Inner thighs
Muscles used: Adductors

PHASE 1

1 Lie on your back and press your lower back into the floor.

2 Relax your arms close to your sides, palms down.

3 Relax your head and shoulders and pull your abdominals in. Flex your toes toward you and extend your legs upward.

> **PERSONAL TRAINER'S TIP**
>
> A small pillow under your head or buttocks can help stop your lower back arching.

PHASE 2

4 Breathe in as you open your legs to a comfortable V, leading with your heels and keeping your feet flexed and legs as straight as you can.

5 Hold briefly at the end of your range of movement, then breathe out as you slowly close your legs. Keep your lower back on the floor.

Make your inner thigh muscles do the work

Note: Depending on your range of movement, you may find the intermediate exercise opposite easier to work at the beginning.

INTERMEDIATE INNER THIGH RAISES
Areas worked: Inner thighs
Muscles used: Adductors

PHASE 1

1 Lie on your right side with your back straight, hips square and feet together.

2 Keep your head, shoulders, knees and ankles aligned. Pull your abdominals in.

3 Place your left leg on the floor at right angles to your body. Keep your right leg straight and flex your foot so that your toes are toward you.

4 Rest your head on your right hand. Place your left hand on the floor in front of you for support. Breathe in.

PHASE 2

5 Breathe out as you slowly raise your right leg as high as is comfortable.

6 Keep your leg straight and foot parallel to the floor.

7 Hold briefly, then breathe in as you lower your leg so that your foot is about 5cm (2in) from the floor and still parallel to it.

8 Complete a set, then turn to your left side and repeat using your left leg.

WEEKS	MEN					WOMEN				
	1–2	3–4	5–6	7–8	9–10	1–2	3–4	5–6	7–8	9–10
BEG.	8x1	12x1	8x2	12x2	10x3	8x1	12x1	8x2	12x2	10x3
INTER.	8x2	12x2	8x3	12x3	16x2	8x2	12x2	8x3	12x3	16x2
ADV.	8x3	12x3	8x4	12x4	16x3	8x3	12x3	8x4	12x4	16x3
EXP.	8x4	12x4	8x4	12x4	10x5	8x4	12x4	8x4	12x4	16x4

STRENGTH • Legs

ADVANCED & EXPERT INNER THIGH RAISES
Areas worked: Inner thighs
Muscles used: Adductors

PHASE 1

1 Fasten securely ankle weights appropriate to your level.

2 Lie on your right side with your back flat and hips square.

3 Keep your head, shoulders, knees and ankles aligned. Pull your abdominals in.

4 Keep your right leg straight. Flex your foot so that your toes are pointing forward.

5 Place your left leg on the floor at right angles to your body.

6 Rest your right forearm and hand and your left hand on the floor for support. Breathe in.

PHASE 2

7 Breathe out as you slowly raise your right leg as high as is comfortable with your foot parallel to the floor.

8 Hold briefly, then breathe in as you lower your leg so that your foot is about 5cm (2in) above the floor and still parallel to it.

9 Complete a set, then turn to your left side and repeat using your left leg.

Note: Many gyms have cable (pulley) or hip adductor machines that also work the inner thigh muscles.

WEEKS	MEN					WOMEN				
	1–2	3–4	5–6	7–8	9–10	1–2	3–4	5–6	7–8	9–10
BEG.	8x1	12x1	8x2	12x2	10x3	8x1	12x1	8x2	12x2	10x3
INTER.	8x2	12x2	8x3	12x3	16x2	8x2	12x2	8x3	12x3	16x2
ADV.	8x3	12x3	8x4	12x4	16x3	8x3	12x3	8x4	12x4	16x3
EXP.	8x4	12x4	8x4	12x4	10x5	8x4	12x4	8x4	12x4	16x4

BEGINNERS' OUTER THIGH RAISES

Areas worked: Outer thighs
Muscles used: Abductors

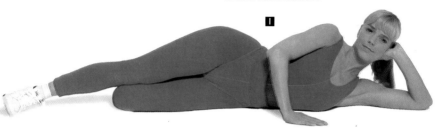

PHASE 1

1 Lie on your left side with your back straight, hips square and feet together.

2 Keep your head, shoulders, knees and ankles aligned. Pull your abdominals in.

3 Bend your left knee at right angles for support.

4 Bend your left elbow and support your head on your left hand.

5 Put your right hand on the floor in front of you for support. Lean slightly forward so that your right hip doesn't roll backward. Breathe in.

PHASE 2

6 Keep your right leg straight with your knee facing forward and foot flexed.

7 Breathe out as you slowly raise your right leg, leading with the outer edge of your foot. Keep your leg straight.

8 Hold briefly, then breathe in as you lower your leg: stop when your foot is about 5cm (2in) from the floor.

9 Complete a set, then turn to your right side and repeat using your left leg.

WEEKS	MEN					WOMEN				
	1–2	3–4	5–6	7–8	9–10	1–2	3–4	5–6	7–8	9–10
BEG.	8x1	12x1	8x2	12x2	10x3	8x1	12x1	8x2	12x2	10x3
INTER.	8x2	12x2	8x3	12x3	16x2	8x2	12x2	8x3	12x3	16x2
ADV.	8x3	12x3	8x4	12x4	16x3	8x3	12x3	8x4	12x4	16x3
EXP.	8x4	12x4	8x4	12x4	10x5	8x4	12x4	8x4	12x4	16x4

STRENGTH • Legs

INTERMEDIATE OUTER THIGH RAISES
Areas worked: Outer thighs
Muscles used: Abductors

PHASE 1

1 Stand with your right side facing, and about 60cm (2ft) away from, a wall. Rest your right hand on the wall and your left on your hip.

2 Keep your head up, back straight, chest lifted and abdominals pulled in.

3 Make sure your hips are square to the front and your feet are hip width apart. Keep your buttocks tight.

4 Bend your knees slightly. Breathe in.

PHASE 2

5 Breathe out as you slowly raise your left leg, keeping your leg straight and foot flexed.

6 Don't raise your leg too high. If you do, your hip may roll backward.

7 Hold briefly, then breathe in as you lower your leg: stop when your foot is about 5cm (2in) from the floor. Try to keep the movement smooth.

8 Complete a set, then repeat with your left side facing the wall, raising your right leg.

ADVANCED & EXPERT OUTER THIGH RAISES

Areas worked: Outer thighs
Muscles used: Abductors

PHASE 1

1 Fasten securely ankle weights appropriate to your level.

2 Follow the directions for phase 1 of the intermediate outer thigh raise opposite.

> **PERSONAL TRAINER'S TIP**
>
> It is important to keep your hips forward: if they roll backward, you will be working your hip flexors rather than your abductors. Concentrate on the muscles you are working.

PHASE 2

3 Breathe out as you slowly raise your left leg, keeping your leg straight and your foot flexed.

4 Don't raise your leg too high. If you do, your hip may roll backward,

5 Hold briefly, then breathe in as you gently lower your leg: stop when your foot is about 5cm (2in) from the floor.

6 Try to keep the movement smooth, not jerky.

7 Complete a set, then repeat with your left side to the wall, raising your right leg.

	MEN					WOMEN				
WEEKS	1–2	3–4	5–6	7–8	9–10	1–2	3–4	5–6	7–8	9–10
BEG.	8x1	12x1	8x2	12x2	10x3	8x1	12x1	8x2	12x2	10x3
INTER.	8x2	12x2	8x3	12x3	16x2	8x2	12x2	8x3	12x3	16x2
ADV.	8x3	12x3	8x4	12x4	16x3	8x3	12x3	8x4	12x4	16x3
EXP.	8x4	12x4	8x4	12x4	10x5	8x4	12x4	8x4	12x4	16x4

STRENGTH•Legs

BEGINNERS' BOTTOM RAISES Areas worked: Buttocks
Muscles used: Gluteals

PHASE
1 Lie face down with your hips pressed into the floor, your abdominals in and pelvis tilted forward.

2 Rest your head on your left forearm and extend your right arm out in front of you with your palm flat on the floor.

3 Keep your legs straight, knees parallel to each other and buttocks tight.

4 Check that your head is in line with your spine. Flex your left foot and breathe in.

Keep your hips pressed into the floor

PHASE 2
5 Breathe out as you raise your left foot as high as is comfortable without arching your back: lead with your heel.

6 Keep your hips on the floor.

7 Hold briefly, then lower your leg until your toes touch the floor.

8 Complete a set with your left leg, then repeat using your right leg.

INTERMEDIATE & ADVANCED BOTTOM RAISES
Areas worked: Buttocks Muscles used: Gluteals

1 At advanced level only, fasten appropriate ankle weights securely.

2 Stand facing, and about 60cm (2ft) away from, a wall. Rest your hands on the wall.

3 Keep your back straight, chest lifted and abdominals in.

4 Check that your hips are square to the front with your pelvis tilted forward. Flex your left foot and breathe in.

5 Breathe out as you raise your foot. Lead with your heel and stop when you feel your hip start to turn outward.

6 Hold briefly, then breathe in as you lower your leg to the floor.

7 Complete a set with your left leg, then repeat using your right leg.

EXPERT BOTTOM RAISES

Areas worked: Buttocks
Muscles used: Gluteals

PHASE

1 Fasten securely ankle weights appropriate to your level.

2 Kneel on all fours with your knees slightly more than hip width apart.

3 Make sure that your arms are directly beneath your shoulders with your palms flat on the floor and fingers pointing forward.

4 Keep your back flat, hips square to the floor, abdominals pulled in and head in line with your spine.

5 Extend your right leg out behind you with your foot flexed. Breathe in.

PHASE 2

6 Breathe out as you raise your right leg to hip height. Keep your leg straight and toes pointing toward the floor.

7 Hold briefly, then breathe in as you lower your leg until your toes touch the floor.

8 Complete a set with your right leg, then repeat using your left leg.

	MEN					WOMEN				
WEEKS	1–2	3–4	5–6	7–8	9–10	1–2	3–4	5–6	7–8	9–10
BEG.	8x1	12x1	8x2	12x2	10x3	8x1	12x1	8x2	12x2	10x3
INTER.	8x2	12x2	8x3	12x3	16x2	8x2	12x2	8x3	12x3	16x2
ADV.	8x3	12x3	8x4	12x4	16x3	8x3	12x3	8x4	12x4	16x3
EXP.	8x4	12x4	8x4	12x4	10x5	8x4	12x4	8x4	12x4	16x4

SAFETY TIP

If you feel any discomfort in your lower back, stop. You may be lifting your leg too high or lifting too heavy a weight. Check posture or weight.

STRENGTH • Legs

BEGINNERS' CALF RAISES Areas worked: Calves Muscles used: Gastrocnemius

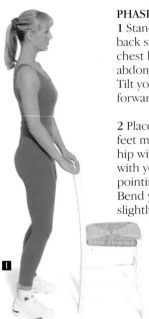

PHASE 1

1 Stand with your back straight, chest lifted and abdominals in. Tilt your pelvis forward.

2 Place your feet more than hip width apart with your toes pointing forward. Bend your knees slightly. Keep your hips square to the front and knees in line with your feet.

3 Look forward and rest your hands on the back of a chair for support.

4 Check that your head is in line with your spine. Breathe in.

PHASE 2

5 Breathe out as you press up on to the balls of your feet.

6 Hold briefly, squeezing your calf muscles.

7 Breathe in as you slowly lower your heels back to the floor.

PERSONAL TRAINER'S TIP

Don't let your ankles roll to the sides as you press up: this puts your ankle tendons and ligaments under stress.

	MEN					WOMEN				
WEEKS	1–2	3–4	5–6	7–8	9–10	1–2	3–4	5–6	7–8	9–10
BEG.	8x1	12x1	8x2	12x2	10x3	8x1	12x1	8x2	12x2	10x3
INTER.	8x2	12x2	8x3	12x3	16x2	8x2	12x2	8x3	12x3	16x2
ADV.	8x3	12x3	8x4	12x4	16x3	8x3	12x3	8x4	12x4	16x3
EXP.	8x4	12x4	8x4	12x4	10x5	8x4	12x4	8x4	12x4	16x4

INTERMEDIATE CALF RAISES   Areas worked: Calves
Muscles used: Gastrocnemius

PHASE 1
1 Stand on a block of wood facing, and about 30cm (1ft) away from, a wall. Let your heels hang over the back of the block.

2 Keep your back straight and tilt your pelvis forward.

3 Bend your knees slightly and keep your hips square to the front.

4 Rest your hands on the wall and look forward.

PHASE 2
5 Check that the balls of your feet are resting firmly on the block. Breathe in.

6 Breathe out as you press up on to the balls of your feet.

7 Hold briefly, squeezing your calf muscles.

PHASE 3
8 Breathe in as you lower down, pointing your heels at the floor. This phase stretches the muscle.

ADVANCED & EXPERT CALF RAISES
Areas worked: Calves   Muscles used: Gastrocnemius

PHASE 1
1 At expert level only, fasten ankle weights securely. Follow the directions for phase 1 of the intermediate calf raise above.

PHASE 2
2 Keep the ball of your left foot on the block with your toes forward.

3 Put your right foot behind your left ankle and breathe in.

4 Breathe out as you press up on to the ball of your left foot. Keep your foot facing forward.

5 Hold briefly, squeezing into your calf muscle.

6 Breathe in as you lower your heel to the floor.

7 Complete a set with your left leg, then repeat using your right leg.

Note: To increase the calf raise, use the intermediate exercise, holding dumbbells on your shoulders.

STRENGTH • Shoulders

BEGINNERS' WALL PRESS UPS
Areas worked: Shoulders, chest, back of arms
Muscles used: Anterior deltoids, pectorals, triceps

PHASE 1
1 Stand facing, and about 60cm (2ft) away from, a wall, with your feet hip width apart.

2 Keep your back straight, chest lifted and abdominals in. Keep your hips square to the front and tilt your pelvis forward.

3 Place your hands flat on the wall, in line with your shoulders and shoulder width apart. Point your fingers upward.

4 Keep your head in line with your spine and look forward.

PHASE 2
5 Breathe in as you bend at the elbows and lean toward the wall. Keep your back flat and legs straight.

6 Aim to touch the wall with your nose. Try not to arch your back.

7 Hold briefly, then breathe out as you press away from the wall, using your arms.

8 Pause briefly between repetitions.

WEEKS	MEN					WOMEN				
	1–2	3–4	5–6	7–8	9–10	1–2	3–4	5–6	7–8	9–10
BEG.	8x1	12x1	8x2	12x2	10x3	8x1	12x1	8x2	12x2	10x3
INTER.	8x2	12x2	8x3	12x3	16x2	8x2	12x2	8x3	12x3	16x2
ADV.	8x3	12x3	8x4	12x4	16x4	8x3	12x3	8x4	12x4	16x3
EXP.	8x4	12x4	16x4	18x4	20x5	8x4	10x4	12x4	16x4	20x4

INTERMEDIATE BOX PRESS UPS

Areas worked: Shoulders, chest, back of arms
Muscles used: Anterior deltoids, pectorals, triceps

PHASE 1

1 Kneel in the box position (see p. 163), with your knees hip width apart.

2 Check that your arms are directly in line with your shoulders with your fingers pointing forward.

3 Keep your back flat, abdominals pulled in and head in line with your spine.

> **SAFETY TIP**
>
> Don't crane your neck forward in an effort to press your chest nearer to the floor: this doesn't help your press up in any way – it simply puts strain on your neck.

Don't lock your elbows

PHASE 2

4 Breathe in as you bend your elbows and lower your upper body to the floor. Aim to touch the floor with your nose.

5 Hold briefly, then breathe out as you press up to the start position, using your arms. Keep your shoulders in line with your arms.

6 Don't lean backward as you press up.

7 Try not to rest between repetitions.

STRENGTH • Shoulders

ADVANCED THREE-QUARTER PRESS UPS
Areas worked: Front of shoulders, chest, back of arms **Muscles used:** Anterior deltoids, pectorals, triceps

PHASE 1
1 Lie face down with your hands directly in line with your shoulders, elbows bent and palms flat on the floor.

2 Place your knees hip width apart. Bend your knees and cross your feet at the ankles. Raise your feet off the floor.

3 Lean your body weight forward so that it is directly above your hands.

4 Keep your back flat, abdominals in and head in line with your spine. Keep your chin in line with your chest. Breathe in.

PHASE 2
5 Breathe out as you press upward, using your arms. Don't lock your elbows.

6 Hold briefly, then breathe in as you lower your upper body toward the floor. Your chest should touch the floor.

7 Try not to rest between repetitions.

Note: The sets and reps chart for this exercise appears on p. 102.

Don't hollow your back as you press up: keep it flat

EXPERT FULL PRESS UPS
Areas worked: Front of shoulders, chest, back of arms
Muscles used: Anterior deltoids, pectorals, triceps

PHASE 1
1 Lie face down with your feet hip width apart, hands directly in line with your shoulders and palms flat on the floor.

2 Press up on to your toes and hands.

3 Keep your back flat, head in line with your spine, abdominals in and chin in line with your chest.

PHASE 2
4 Breathe in as you lower your chest to the floor.

5 Hold briefly, then breathe out as you push up. Don't lock your elbows.

6 Don't rest between repetitions.

Note: To extend a press up, support your feet on a bench and lower your chest to the floor.

LATERAL RAISES   Areas worked: Shoulders   Muscles used: Medial deltoids

PHASE ◼1
1 Dead lift a set of dumbbells to the front of your thighs (see p. 76).

2 Stand with your back straight, chest lifted and abdominals in.

3 Place your feet hip width apart. Tilt your pelvis forward and keep your hips ·square to the front. Bend your knees slightly.

4 Bring your hands to the front of your thighs, with your palms facing each other. Bend your elbows and breathe in.

PHASE ◼2
5 Breathe out as you extend your arms out to the sides in a semi-circle, leading with your elbows and knuckles.

6 Keeping your arms aligned, raise the weights to shoulder height (not above). Don't lock your elbows.

7 Turn your wrists up, keeping them straight: at their greatest height, the weights should be parallel to the floor.

■1

8 Hold briefly, then breathe in as you lower the dumbbells to the front of your thighs.

SAFETY TIP

Before progressing to a heavier weight, be sure that you are ready to lift more. Increasing weights too soon can cause your technique to suffer and may lead to injury.

■2

WEEKS	MEN					WOMEN				
	1–2	3–4	5–6	7–8	9–10	1–2	3–4	5–6	7–8	9–10
BEG.	8x1	12x1	8x2	12x2	10x3	8x1	12x1	8x2	12x2	10x3
INTER.	8x2	12x2	8x3	12x3	10x4	8x2	12x2	8x3	12x3	10x4
ADV.	8x3	12x3	8x4	12x4	10x4	8x3	12x3	8x4	12x4	10x4
EXP.	8x4	12x4	8x4	12x4	8x5	8x4	12x4	8x4	12x4	10x5

STRENGTH · Shoulders

DUMBBELL PRESSES Areas worked: Front of shoulders, shoulders, upper back, back of arms

Muscles used: Anterior deltoids, deltoids, trapezius, triceps

PHASE ▮

1 Dead lift a set of dumbbells to your sides (see p. 76).

2 Stand with your back straight, chest lifted and abdominals in. Place your feet hip width apart. Tilt your pelvis forward.

3 Lift the weights to shoulder height. Keep your palms facing forward and wrists straight.

4 Keep your head in line with your spine and look forward. Breathe in.

PHASE ▮

5 Breathe out as you bend your elbows slightly and press the dumbbells to arm's length above your head. Lead with your knuckles, keeping them pointing at the ceiling.

6 Pause briefly, then breathe in as you lower the dumbbells to shoulder height.

7 When you have completed all your sets, lower the dumbbells to the floor (see p. 76).

Note: This exercise can also be performed sitting on the end of a bench, which makes it more demanding. Alternatively, lift one dumbbell then the other.

▮

SAFETY TIP

Keep your back straight during the lift: if you lean backward you risk straining your lower back.

	MEN					WOMEN				
WEEKS	1–2	3–4	5–6	7–8	9–10	1–2	3–4	5–6	7–8	9–10
BEG.	8x1	12x1	8x2	12x2	10x3	8x1	12x1	8x2	12x2	10x3
INTER.	8x2	12x2	8x3	12x3	10x4	8x2	12x2	8x3	12x3	10x4
ADV.	8x3	12x3	8x4	12x4	10x4	8x3	12x3	8x4	12x4	10x4
EXP.	8x4	12x4	8x4	12x4	8x5	8x4	12x4	8x4	12x4	10x5

▮

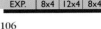

MACHINE SHOULDER PRESSES

Areas worked: Shoulders, upper back, back of arms

Muscles used: Anterior deltoids, deltoids, trapezius, triceps

PHASE 1

1 Check the pin in the stack and the height and depth of the seat (see p. 75).

2 Sit with your back straight, chest lifted and head in line with your spine. Pull your abdominals in tightly.

3 Take an overhand grip on the bar, with your hands 1½ times shoulder width apart or slightly wider (remember the muscles you are working).

4 Make sure that the bar is slightly forward of, and at about the same height as, your shoulders.

1

2

5 Keep your elbows down and wrists in line with your knuckles. Point your knuckles up.

6 Rest your feet flat on the foot space of the machine or, if there isn't one, on the floor. Breathe in.

PHASE 2

7 Breathe out as you slowly press the bar upward. Don't arch your back: make your shoulders and arms do the work.

8 Press the bar to arm's length: don't lock your elbows.

9 Pause briefly, then breathe in as you lower the bar, leading with your elbows.

10 Don't let the weight touch the stack between repetitions.

PERSONAL TRAINER'S TIP

If pressing up is difficult lean slightly forward as you press. Keep your torso rigid.

WEEKS	MEN					WOMEN				
	1–2	3–4	5–6	7–8	9–10	1–2	3–4	5–6	7–8	9–10
BEG.	8x1	12x1	8x2	12x2	10x3	8x1	12x1	8x2	12x2	10x3
INTER.	8x2	12x2	8x3	12x3	10x4	8x2	12x2	8x3	12x3	10x4
ADV.	8x3	12x3	8x4	12x4	10x4	8x3	12x3	8x4	12x4	10x4
EXP.	8x4	12x4	8x4	12x4	8x5	8x4	12x4	8x4	12x4	10x5

STRENGTH • Shoulders

PRESS BEHIND NECK **Areas worked:** Shoulders, upper back, back of arms
Muscles used: Anterior deltoids, trapezius, triceps

PHASE 1

1 Dead lift a barbell (see p. 76) and clean it to the receive position (see pp. 120–21).

2 Bend at your knees and press the bar above your head, then lower it to your shoulders (not your neck).

3 Place your feet shoulder width apart. Stand with your back straight, chest lifted and abdominals in. Tilt your pelvis forward.

4 Widen your grip so that your hands are 1½ times shoulder width apart.

5 Keep your elbows pointing down and wrists in line with your knuckles. Point your knuckles up.

6 Keep your head in line with your spine and look forward. Breathe in.

PHASE 2

7 Breathe out as you press the bar to arm's length, leading with your knuckles. Don't lock your elbows.

8 Hold briefly, then breathe in as you lower the barbell to your shoulders: lead with your elbows.

9 Don't rest the bar on your shoulders between repetitions.

10 When you have completed all your sets, narrow your hand grip to shoulder width and lower the barbell to the floor (see p. 76).

Note: This exercise is suitable at advanced and expert levels only. Use the repetitions chart for bent forward lateral raises opposite.

Don't lock your elbows

108

BENT FORWARD LATERAL RAISES   **Areas worked:** Back of shoulders, upper back
Muscles used: Posterior deltoids, rhomboideus major

PHASE 1

1 Place a set of dumbbells at the foot of a bench.

2 Sit on the end of the bench with your feet hip width apart, back flat, abdominals pulled in and chest toward your knees.

3 Keep your head in line with your spine, and look down.

4 Hold the dumbbells directly in line with your shoulders. Keep your palms facing each other with your elbows slightly bent and wrists straight. Breathe in.

SAFETY TIP

This exercise can also be performed standing, but you must ensure that your back is flat and your shoulders are doing the work. If not you risk putting strain on your lower back.

PHASE 2

5 Breathe out as you raise the dumbbells in a semi-circle out to the sides. Lead with your elbows and knuckles and stop when the weights are level with your shoulders. Keep your elbows slightly bent.

6 Hold briefly, then breathe in as you lower the weights to the start position.

7 Don't jerk the movement; keep the repetitions smooth.

		MEN					WOMEN			
WEEKS	1–2	3–4	5–6	7–8	9–10	1–2	3–4	5–6	7–8	9–10
BEG.	–	–	–	–	–	–	–	–	–	–
INTER.	–	–	–	–	–	–	–	–	–	–
ADV.	8x3	12x3	8x4	12x4	10x4	8x3	12x3	8x4	12x4	10x4
EXP.	8x4	12x4	8x4	12x4	8x5	8x4	12x4	8x4	12x4	10x5

STRENGTH • Shoulders

UPRIGHT ROWS

Areas worked: Upper back, front of shoulders, front of arms
Muscles used: Trapezius, anterior deltoids, triceps

PHASE ▮

1 Dead lift a barbell to the front of your thighs (see p. 76).

2 Stand with your back straight, chest lifted and abdominals in. Tilt your pelvis forward.

3 Place your feet shoulder width apart and bend your knees slightly. Keep your hips square to the front.

4 Narrow your hand grip to about 10cm (4in) apart. Keep your wrists straight and relax your shoulders. Breathe in.

PERSONAL TRAINER'S TIP

An alternative way to work this exercise is to substitute dumbbells for the barbell. Use one in each hand with your hands close together. Raise the dumbbells together, leading with your elbows. Keep your elbows high and your wrists straight.

Don't allow your hips to come forward

PHASE ▮

5 Breathe out as you draw the barbell toward your chest, leading with your elbows.

6 Keep the bar close to your body, with your elbows high.

7 Hold briefly, then breathe in as you lower the bar back to the start position.

8 When you have completed all your sets, widen your grip so that your hands are shoulder width apart and lower the barbell to the floor (see p. 76).

WEEKS	MEN					WOMEN				
	1–2	3–4	5–6	7–8	9–10	1–2	3–4	5–6	7–8	9–10
BEG.	–	–	–	–	–	–	–	–	–	–
INTER.	–	–	–	–	–	–	–	–	–	–
ADV.	8x3	12x3	8x4	12x4	10x4	8x3	12x3	8x4	12x4	10x4
EXP.	8x4	12x4	8x4	12x4	8x5	8x4	12x4	8x4	12x4	10x5

FORWARD RAISES

Areas worked: Front of shoulders, chest
Muscles used: Anterior deltoid, pectorals

PHASE 1

1 Dead lift a set of dumbbells to your sides (see p. 76).

2 Stand with your back straight, chest lifted and abdominals in. Tilt your pelvis forward.

3 Place your feet hip width apart. Bend your knees slightly. Bring the dumbbells to the front of your thighs with your palms facing your body and your wrists straight. Breathe in.

PHASE 2

4 Breathe out as you raise the dumbbells to shoulder height (not above). Lead with your knuckles and try not to lock your elbows.

5 Hold briefly, then breathe in as you lower the weights. Keep them under control.

6 When you have completed all your sets, lower the dumbbells to the floor (see p. 76).

PERSONAL TRAINER'S TIP

You can also work this exercise using a partner as resistance. As you push up, get your partner to push down on your hands.

WEEKS	MEN					WOMEN				
	1–2	3–4	5–6	7–8	9–10	1–2	3–4	5–6	7–8	9–10
BEG.	–	–	–	–	–	–	–	–	–	–
INTER.	8x2	12x2	8x3	12x3	10x4	8x2	12x2	8x3	12x3	10x4
ADV.	8x3	12x3	8x4	12x4	10x4	8x3	12x3	8x4	12x4	10x4
EXP.	8x4	12x4	8x4	12x4	8x5	8x4	12x4	8x4	12x4	10x5

STRENGTH • Back

BACK RAISES Areas worked: Lower back, middle back **Muscles used:** Erector spinae

PHASE ▌
1 Lie face down with your legs extended, feet together and toes pointing toward the floor. Stretch out your arms over your head, keeping them on the floor.

2 Keep your forehead on the floor and head in line with your spine throughout.

3 Pull your abdominals in and press your hips into the floor.

4 Keep your buttocks tight. Breathe in.

PHASE ▌
5 Breathe out as you raise your right arm, leading with your fingers, and left leg, leading with the heel, to a comfortable height.

6 Hold briefly at the top of the movement, then breathe in as you slowly return your arm and leg to the floor.

7 Repeat using your right leg and left arm. Be sure to work both sides equally.

Keep your head in line with your spine and don't drop your chin

SAFETY TIP
Don't jerk your leg and arm up in an attempt to get them higher. This puts strain on your back.

WEEKS	MEN					WOMEN				
	1–2	3–4	5–6	7–8	9–10	1–2	3–4	5–6	7–8	9–10
BEG.	8x1	12x1	8x2	12x2	10x3	8x1	12x1	8x2	12x2	10x3
INTER.	8x2	12x2	8x3	12x3	16x2	8x2	12x2	8x3	12x3	16x2
ADV.	–	–	–	–	–	–	–	–	–	–
EXP.	–	–	–	–	–	–	–	–	–	–

SHOULDER SHRUGS **Areas worked**: Upper back **Muscles used**: Trapezius, rhomboids

PHASE 1

1 Dead lift a set of dumbbells to your sides (see p. 76), with your palms facing each other.

2 Stand with your back straight, chest lifted and abdominals in. Tilt your pelvis forward.

3 Place your feet hip width apart and bend your knees slightly.

4 Keep your head in line with your spine and look forward.

5 Relax your shoulders and breathe in.

PHASE 2

6 Breathe out as you slowly raise your shoulders, then roll them back. Keep the dumbbells close to your body.

7 Hold briefly, then breathe in as you lower your shoulders to the start position.

	MEN					WOMEN				
WEEKS	1–2	3–4	5–6	7–8	9–10	1–2	3–4	5–6	7–8	9–10
BEG.	–	–	–	–	–	–	–	–	–	–
INTER.	8x2	12x2	8x3	12x3	10x4	8x2	12x2	8x3	12x3	10x4
ADV.	8x3	12x3	8x4	12x4	10x4	8x3	12x3	8x4	12x4	10x4
EXP.	8x4	12x4	8x4	12x4	8x5	8x4	12x4	8x4	12x4	10x5

STRENGTH • Back

BEGINNERS' LOWER BACK RAISES   Areas worked: Lower back   Muscles used: Erector spinae

PHASE ▮

1 Lie face down with your legs extended, feet together and toes pointing toward the floor.

2 Press your hips into the floor, pull your abdominals in and tilt your pelvis forward.

3 Keep your head in line with your spine and chin down.

4 Place your hands on your buttocks with your palms flat. Breathe in.

Keep your hips pressed into the floor

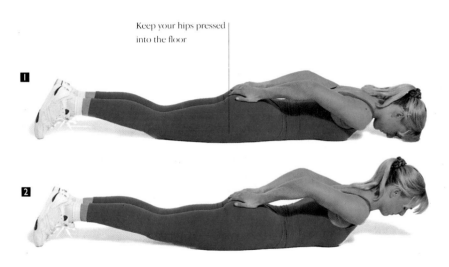

PHASE ▮

5 Breathe out as you raise your upper body off the floor: keep the movement smooth.

6 Keep your hips pressed into the floor. Hold briefly, then breathe in as you slowly lower your upper body.

SAFETY TIP

If you feel discomfort at the top of the movement, you are raising too high. Keep it under control.

WEEKS	MEN					WOMEN				
	1–2	3–4	5–6	7–8	9–10	1–2	3–4	5–6	7–8	9–10
BEG.	8x1	12x1	8x2	12x2	10x3	8x1	12x1	8x2	12x2	10x3
INTER.	8x2	12x2	8x3	12x3	16x2	8x2	12x2	8x3	12x3	16x2
ADV.	8x3	12x3	8x4	12x4	16x3	8x3	12x3	8x4	12x4	16x3
EXP.	8x4	12x4	16x4	18x4	20x5	8x4	10x4	12x4	16x4	18x4

INTERMEDIATE & ADVANCED

Follow the
directions for the
beginners'
exercise, except:
4 Place your
hands under
your chin.

EXPERT

Follow the
directions for the
beginners'
exercise, except:
4 Extend your
arms above your
head on the
floor.

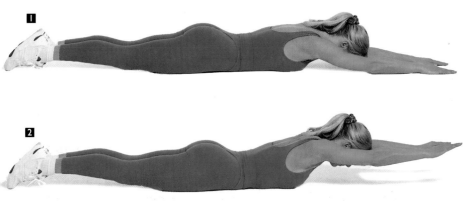

STRENGTH • Back

SINGLE ARM ROWS
Areas worked: Middle back, arms
Muscles used: Latissimus dorsi, biceps

PHASE **1**

1 Stand sideways on to a bench, and place a dumbbell on the floor within arm's reach.

2 Place your left knee and left hand on the bench, with your hand directly in line with your shoulder. Don't lock your elbow.

3 Bend your right knee slightly and keep your foot flat on the floor.

4 Take an overhand grip on the dumbbell and lift it off the floor, keeping your arm straight.

5 Keep your back flat, abdominals in, head in line with your spine and hips square to the floor. Breathe in.

PHASE **2**

6 Breathe out as you pull the dumbbell, under control, toward your chest. Lead with your elbow and keep your wrist straight. Keep your elbow close to your body.

7 Hold briefly, then breathe in as you lower the dumbbell to arm's length. Don't lock your elbow.

8 Complete a set with your right arm, then repeat using your left arm with your right knee and hand on the bench.

Note: To help get the right action for this exercise, imagine you are sawing wood.

1

Keep your elbow close to your body throughout

2

	MEN					WOMEN				
WEEKS	1–2	3–4	5–6	7–8	9–10	1–2	3–4	5–6	7–8	9–10
BEG.	–	–	–	–	–	–	–	–	–	–
INTER.	8x2	12x2	8x3	12x3	10x4	8x2	12x2	8x3	12x3	10x4
ADV.	8x3	12x3	8x4	12x4	10x4	8x3	12x3	8x4	12x4	10x4
EXP.	8x4	12x4	8x4	12x4	8x5	8x4	12x4	8x4	12x4	10x5

MACHINE LAT PULL DOWNS Areas worked: Back, arms
Muscles used: Latissimus dorsi, biceps, brachialis

PHASE 1

1 Check the pin in the stack and the height and depth of the seat (see p. 75).

2 Sit with your back straight, chest lifted and abdominals in. Keep your head in line with your spine.

3 Take an overhand grip on the bar with your hands 1½ times shoulder width apart. Make sure that your knuckles are facing upward and your wrists are straight.

4 Check that the pulley cable is vertical and breathe in.

1   **2**

PHASE 2

5 Breathe out as you slowly pull the bar down toward the nape of your neck, leading with your elbows. Keep the movement under control.

6 Tilt your head slightly forward so that you don't hit your head when you pull the bar down.

7 Keep the bar and cable close to your body and your wrists straight throughout.

8 Hold briefly, then breathe in as you return the bar to the start position. Don't lock your elbows.

Note: This is an excellent exercise for developing the width of your back.

PERSONAL TRAINER'S TIP

A partner may be able to help with the last pulls. If you work alone, watch how much weight you have on the stack.

	MEN					WOMEN				
WEEKS	1–2	3–4	5–6	7–8	9–10	1–2	3–4	5–6	7–8	9–10
BEG.	8x1	12x1	8x2	12x2	10x3	8x1	12x1	8x2	12x2	10x3
INTER.	8x2	12x2	8x3	12x3	10x4	8x2	12x2	8x3	12x3	10x4
ADV.	8x3	12x3	8x4	12x4	10x4	8x3	12x3	8x4	12x4	10x4
EXP.	8x4	12x4	8x4	12x4	8x5	8x4	12x4	8x4	12x4	10x5

STRENGTH • Back

BARBELL ROWS **Areas worked**: Back of arms, front of arms
Muscles used: Latissimus dorsi, biceps, brachialis

PHASE **1**

1 Stand with your feet slightly more than hip width apart and toes facing forward. Place a barbell at your feet.

2 Keep your back flat, chest lifted and abdominals in. Bend your knees and bend forward from your hips.

3 Keep your head in line with your spine and look forward.

4 Take an overhand grip on the barbell with your hands shoulder width apart and breathe in.

PHASE **2**

5 Breathe out as you slowly draw the barbell toward your upper abdomen (just below your rib cage). Lead with your elbows and keep your back flat.

6 Hold briefly, then breathe in as you return the barbell to the floor.

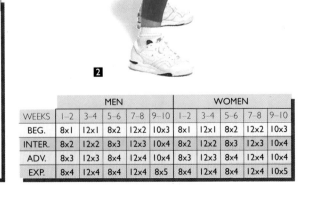

Keep your knees bent _____

1

2

SAFETY TIP

Only do barbell rows at advanced and expert levels. Don't use a weight that is too heavy. This causes you to sacrifice your technique which could lead to injuries.

	MEN					WOMEN				
WEEKS	1–2	3–4	5–6	7–8	9–10	1–2	3–4	5–6	7–8	9–10
BEG.	8x1	12x1	8x2	12x2	10x3	8x1	12x1	8x2	12x2	10x3
INTER.	8x2	12x2	8x3	12x3	10x4	8x2	12x2	8x3	12x3	10x4
ADV.	8x3	12x3	8x4	12x4	10x4	8x3	12x3	8x4	12x4	10x4
EXP.	8x4	12x4	8x4	12x4	8x5	8x4	12x4	8x4	12x4	10x5

MACHINE SEATED ROWS   Areas worked: Back, arms

Muscles used: Latissimus dorsi, biceps, brachialis

Note: This is the same exercise as the barbell rows opposite, worked in the gym.

PHASE **1**
1 Sit with your feet on the foot platform. If there is no lip for your heels, make sure your feet are in the centre of the platform so that there is no chance of them slipping off.

2 Make sure that your feet, ankles, knees and hips are aligned.

3 Take an overhand grip on the bar, with your hands shoulder width apart, wrists straight and knuckles pointing up.

4 Slide back to a position where your back is straight and your knees are slightly bent, but not locked. Pull your abdominals in.

5 Keep your chest lifted, arms extended (don't lock your elbows) and head in line with your spine. Breathe in.

1

PHASE **2**
6 Breathe out as you slowly draw the bar toward your chest: lead with your elbows.

7 Keep your elbows close to your waist and upper body upright.

8 Hold briefly, then breathe in as you return the bar to the start position. Don't let the weight touch the stack.

2

STRENGTH • Back

THE CLEAN   Area worked: Calves, front of thighs, buttocks, upper and lower back, shoulders, arms
Muscles used: Gastrocnemius, quadriceps, gluteals, erector spinae, trapezius, deltoids, biceps, brachialis

PHASE 1
1 Stand as described for phase 1 of the dead lift (see p. 76).

PHASE 2
2 Lift the barbell to the front of your thighs, as described for phases 2 and 3 of the dead lift.

PHASE 3
3 Breathe out as you draw the barbell toward your chest. Lead with your elbows and keep your wrists straight (the upright row, see p. 110).

PHASE 4
4 Hold the bar close to your body in the upright row position, and rise up on to your toes. Keep your elbows high above the bar.

5 Check that your feet are still hip width apart for balance.

PHASE 5
6 Roll your shoulders back and bring your elbows down under the bar and round to the front of your body so that you now have an underhand grip on the barbell. This is the **receive position**.

PHASE 6
7 Hold briefly, then breathe in as you roll your shoulders forward and pull your elbows high above the bar into an upright row.

120

3 6

> ### PERSONAL TRAINER'S TIP
>
> The most effective way to practise this exercise is with a broomstick in front of a mirror, not using heavy weights. Practise the phases individually, then string them together. Start using weights when you are confident of the technique.

4

Keep your hips square to the front throughout

PHASE 7
8 Slowly lower your arms so that you are holding the barbell at arm's length at the front of your thighs. Keep the bar close to your body and don't lock your elbows.

PHASE 8
9 Repeat.

PHASE 9
10 When you have completed all your sets, lower the bar to the floor.

5

Keep your elbows down and knuckles up

	MEN					WOMEN				
WEEKS	1–2	3–4	5–6	7–8	9–10	1–2	3–4	5–6	7–8	9–10
BEG.	–	–	–	–	–	–	–	–	–	–
INTER.	–	–	–	–	–	–	–	–	–	–
ADV.	–	–	–	–	–	–	–	–	–	–
EXP.	8x4	12x4	8x4	12x4	8x5	8x4	12x4	8x4	12x4	10x5

STRENGTH • Chest

EXPERT PRESS UPS **Areas worked**: Chest, back of arms, front of shoulders
Muscles used: Pectorals, triceps, anterior deltoids

PHASE ▮

1 Lie face down with your feet hip width apart.

2 Place your hands out to your sides in line with your shoulders and about 30cm (12in) wider than your shoulders on each side.

3 Make sure that your fingers are pointing straight ahead.

4 Lean your body weight forward so that your chest is slightly in front of your hands.

5 Press up on to your toes and hands. Keep your back flat, abdominals in and head in line with your spine.

▮

PHASE ▮

6 Breathe in as you lower your upper body down.

▮

7 Aim to touch the floor with your chest. Hold briefly, then breathe out as you press back up through your arms.

8 Don't allow your elbow joints to lock or your back to hollow as you press up.

9 Don't rest between repetitions.

PERSONAL TRAINER'S TIP

The press ups on pp. 102–4 can all be performed "wide arm" to emphasize your chest rather than your shoulders. Choose the appropriate start position for your level: beginners (*left*), intermediate (*top right*) and advanced (*bottom right*).

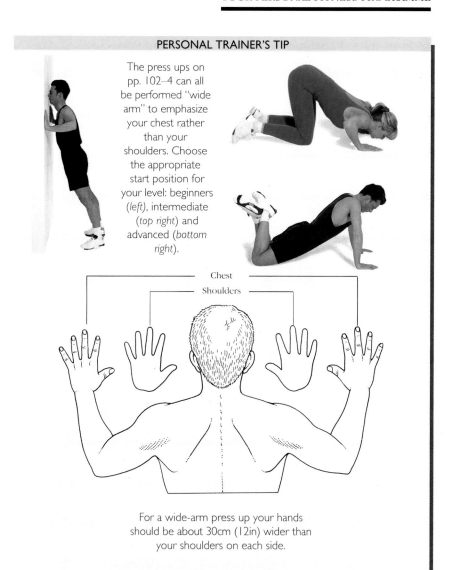

For a wide-arm press up your hands should be about 30cm (12in) wider than your shoulders on each side.

WEEKS	MEN					WOMEN				
	1–2	3–4	5–6	7–8	9–10	1–2	3–4	5–6	7–8	9–10
BEG.	8x1	12x1	8x2	12x2	10x3	8x1	12x1	8x2	12x2	10x3
INTER.	8x2	12x2	8x3	12x3	16x2	8x2	12x2	8x3	12x3	16x2
ADV.	8x3	12x3	8x4	12x4	16x4	8x3	12x3	8x4	12x4	16x3
EXP.	8x4	12x4	16x4	18x4	20x5	8x4	10x4	12x4	16x4	20x4

STRENGTH · Chest

FLAT BENCH PRESSES
Areas worked: Chest, back of arms, front of shoulders
Muscles used: Pectorals, triceps, anterior deltoids

PHASE ▮
1 Lie on your back on a bench with your feet flat on the floor and hip width apart.

2 Keep your lower back as flat on the bench as possible but don't force it out of its natural S curve (put weights or blocks under your feet to raise them if you have trouble keeping your back flat).

3 Check that your head is in line with your spine and that you are square on the bench. Pull your abdominals in.

4 Make sure that the barbell is in the centre of the rack (if your bench doesn't have a rack, dead lift the barbell to your thighs, then sit, then lie down with it at your waist).

5 Take an overhand grip on the barbell, with your hands about 1½ times shoulder width apart, your wrists straight and your knuckles up. Line up the bar at the midline of your chest and breathe in.

6 Breathe out as you press the barbell to arm's length, leading with your knuckles. Don't lock your elbows.

PHASE ▮
7 Hold briefly, then breathe in as you lower the barbell to the midline of your chest, leading with your elbows.

Remember: Don't do exercises lying down using heavy free weights alone if your bench doesn't have a rack. Even if your bench does have a rack it's advisable to work with a partner.

MACHINE BENCH PRESSES

Areas worked: Chest, back of arms, front of shoulders
Muscles used: Pectorals, triceps, anterior deltoids

PHASE ❶

1 Check the pin in the stack and the height of the bench (see p. 75).

2 Lie on your back with your feet flat on the floor and hip width apart.

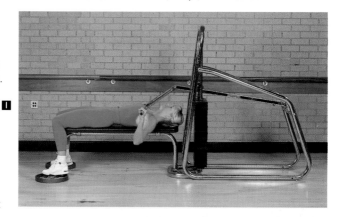

3 Keep your lower back as flat on the bench as possible but don't force it out of its natural S curve (put weights under your feet if you can't keep your back flat).

4 Check that your head is in line with your spine and that you are square on the bench. Pull your abdominals in.

5 Take an overhand grip on the bar with your hands 1½ times shoulder width apart, your wrists straight and knuckles up. Line up the bar at the midline of your chest and breathe in.

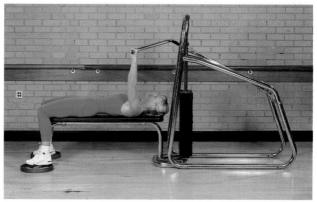

PHASE ❷

6 Breathe out as you press the bar to arm's length. Don't lock your elbows.

7 Hold briefly, then breathe in as you slowly return the bar to your chest: stop short of the weight stack.

8 Try not to rest between repetitions.

WEEKS	MEN					WOMEN				
	1–2	3–4	5–6	7–8	9–10	1–2	3–4	5–6	7–8	9–10
BEG.	8x1	12x1	8x2	12x2	10x3	8x1	12x1	8x2	12x2	10x3
INTER.	8x2	12x2	8x3	12x3	10x4	8x2	12x2	8x3	12x3	10x4
ADV.	8x3	12x3	8x4	12x4	10x4	8x3	12x3	8x4	12x4	10x4
EXP.	8x4	12x4	8x4	12x4	8x5	8x4	12x4	8x4	12x4	10x5

STRENGTH • Chest

INCLINE BENCH PRESSES
Areas worked: Chest, back of arms, front of arms, front of shoulders
Muscles used: Pectorals, triceps, biceps, anterior deltoids

PHASE ■
1 Set a bench in the incline position.

2 Follow the directions for phase 1 of the flat bench presses on p. 124.

PHASE ■
3 Hold briefly, then breathe in as you lower the barbell to your chest, leading with your elbows. Don't lock your elbows.

4 Be sure to keep your wrists straight and keep the barbell in line with the midline of your chest.

5 Try not to rest between repetitions.

Remember: Don't work exercises lying down using heavy free weights alone if your bench doesn't have a rack. Even if your bench does have a rack it's advisable to work with a partner.

	MEN					WOMEN				
WEEKS	1–2	3–4	5–6	7–8	9–10	1–2	3–4	5–6	7–8	9–10
BEG.	–	–	–	–	–	–	–	–	–	–
INTER.	8x2	12x2	8x3	12x3	10x4	8x2	12x2	8x3	12x3	10x4
ADV.	8x3	12x3	8x4	12x4	10x4	8x3	12x3	8x4	12x4	10x4
EXP.	8x4	12x4	8x4	12x4	8x5	8x4	12x4	8x4	12x4	10x5

FLAT BENCH FLIES   Areas worked: Chest, shoulders   Muscles used: Pectorals, anterior deltoids

PHASE 1

1 Dead lift a set of dumbbells to your thighs, then sit on a bench with the weights in your lap.

2 Lie down with your feet flat on the floor and hip width apart.

3 Check that your head is in line with your spine and that you are square on the bench. Pull your abdominals in.

PHASE 2

7 Breathe in as you extend your arms out to the sides: lead with your elbows, keeping them slightly bent.

8 Keep your arms in line with your shoulders and chest. Stop when they are at shoulder level.

4 Keep your lower back pressed into the bench and abdominals in.

5 With an overhand grip on the weights, bring them to your chest.

6 Under control, press the dumbbells to arm's length above you. Slightly bend your elbows and wrists so that your knuckles face each other.

9 Hold briefly, then breathe out as you press your arms back together above your chest.

Note: You can also work incline bench flies. Set the bench in the incline position opposite. Use the repetitions chart below.

1

2

WEEKS	MEN					WOMEN				
	1–2	3–4	5–6	7–8	9–10	1–2	3–4	5–6	7–8	9–10
BEG.	–	–	–	–	–	–	–	–	–	–
INTER.	–	–	–	–	–	–	–	–	–	–
ADV.	8x3	12x3	8x4	12x4	10x4	8x3	12x3	8x4	12x4	10x4
EXP.	8x4	12x4	8x4	12x4	8x5	8x4	12x4	8x4	12x4	10x5

STRENGTH • Chest

MACHINE SEATED PEC DECS   Areas worked: Chest
Muscles used: Pectorals

PHASE 1

1 Check the pin in the stack and the height and depth of the seat. (If the seat is small, you may need an extra pad to keep your shoulders in alignment.)

2 Sit with your back straight, chest lifted and abdominals in. Keep your head in line with your spine.

1

2

3 Put your feet flat on the floor or on the foot roller.

4 Place your forearms flat on the pads, with your hands relaxed. Check that the pads "fit" from your wrists to your elbows: your forearms will be doing the work. Breathe in.

PHASE 2

5 Breathe out as you press your forearms together. Keep the movement under control with your back straight and shoulders and wrists relaxed. Keep your elbows in contact with the pads.

6 When the pads are at the midline of your chest, hold, squeezing deep into your pectorals.

7 Breathe in as you slowly return the pads to the start position.

SAFETY TIP

The temptation in this exercise is to use your wrists, forcing the elbows off the pads. This is a weak area in many people and you risk putting them under severe stress.

	MEN					WOMEN				
WEEKS	1–2	3–4	5–6	7–8	9–10	1–2	3–4	5–6	7–8	9–10
BEG.	8x1	12x1	8x2	12x2	10x3	8x1	12x1	8x2	12x2	10x3
INTER.	8x2	12x2	8x3	12x3	10x4	8x2	12x2	8x3	12x3	10x4
ADV.	8x3	12x3	8x4	12x4	10x4	8x3	12x3	8x4	12x4	10x4
EXP.	8x4	12x4	8x4	12x4	8x5	8x4	12x4	8x4	12x4	10x5

BENT ARM PULLOVERS
Areas worked: Chest, back
Muscles used: Pectorals, latissimus dorsi

PHASE 1

1 Dead lift a dumbbell to your thighs (see p. 76), then sit on a bench with the weight in your lap.

2 Lie with your back as flat as possible on the bench but don't force it out of its natural S curve (put weights under your feet if you can't get your back flat; if that doesn't work, put your feet flat on the bench).

3 Check that your head is in line with your spine and that you are square on the bench. Pull your abdominals in.

4 Raise the dumbbell above your chest, keeping your elbows bent and tucked into your sides. Keep your wrists straight and knuckles pointing up.

PHASE 2

5 Breathe in as you extend the dumbbell over your head toward the floor. Keep your elbows at a 45° angle.

6 Breathe out as you slowly return the weight above your chest, leading with your elbows.

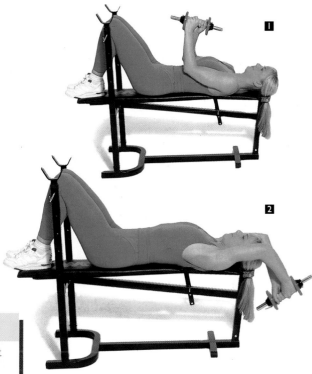

PERSONAL TRAINER'S TIP

This is a good chest builder. As an alternative, use a barbell but take care not to go beyond your natural range of movement.

WEEKS	MEN					WOMEN				
	1–2	3–4	5–6	7–8	9–10	1–2	3–4	5–6	7–8	9–10
BEG.	–	–	–	–	–	–	–	–	–	–
INTER.	–	–	–	–	–	–	–	–	–	–
ADV.	8x3	12x3	8x4	12x4	10x4	8x3	12x3	8x4	12x4	10x4
EXP.	8x4	12x3	8x4	12x4	8x5	8x4	12x4	8x4	12x4	10x5

STRENGTH • Arms

DUMBBELL CURLS Areas worked: Front of arms, forearms
Muscles used: Biceps, brachialis

PHASE 1

1 Take an underhand grip on a set of dumbbells and dead lift them to the front of your thighs (see p. 76).

2 Stand with your feet shoulder width apart and facing forward, and your knees slightly bent.

3 Keep your back straight, chest lifted and abdominals in. Check that your head is in line with your spine.

4 Relax your shoulders and keep your upper arms tucked into your body. Bend your elbows slightly and bring them toward the front of your body for stability.

5 Keep your wrists straight and knuckles facing forward. Breathe in.

PERSONAL TRAINER'S TIP

It is all too easy to let your elbows come forward and away from your body so that you use your back to help with the last couple of difficult repetitions. To avoid this, try pressing your back against a wall or working your right and left arms alternately.

PHASE 2

6 Breathe out as you slowly raise the dumbbells toward your upper arms and shoulders. Keep your upper arms pinned to your body and wrists straight.

7 Hold briefly, then breathe in as you slowly lower the weights to the start position. Try not to overextend your elbows.

	MEN					WOMEN				
WEEKS	1–2	3–4	5–6	7–8	9–10	1–2	3–4	5–6	7–8	9–10
BEG.	8x1	12x1	8x2	12x2	10x3	8x1	12x1	8x2	12x2	10x3
INTER.	8x2	12x2	8x3	12x3	10x4	8x2	12x2	8x3	12x3	10x4
ADV.	8x3	12x3	8x4	12x4	10x4	8x3	12x3	8x4	12x4	10x4
EXP.	8x4	12x4	8x4	12x4	8x5	8x4	12x4	8x4	12x4	10x5

CONCENTRATED CURLS

Areas worked: Front of arms, forearms
Muscles used: Biceps, brachialis

1 With your right hand dead lift a dumbbell to the front of your thigh (see p. 76), then sit on the end of a bench. Place your feet flat on the floor a comfortable distance apart.

2 Pull your abdominals in and, with your back flat, bend forward from the waist. Keep your head in line with your spine.

3 Rest your left forearm on your left thigh. Keep your right wrist straight and place your right elbow on your right inner thigh. Breathe in.

4 Keeping your back flat and wrist straight, breathe out as you slowly raise the dumbbell toward your upper arm and shoulder.

5 Squeezing your biceps, breathe in as you slowly lower the weight to the start position.

SAFETY TIPS

- If you use a weight that is too heavy, you risk straining your back on the last couple of lifts.
- Keep your back flat but don't try to sit upright. Make your abdominals do the work of keeping your torso steady.

6 It is important to keep the dumbbell under control as you raise and lower: place your left hand on the outside of your right arm to help if necessary.

7 Complete a set with your right arm, then repeat, using your left arm.

WEEKS	MEN					WOMEN				
	1–2	3–4	5–6	7–8	9–10	1–2	3–4	5–6	7–8	9–10
BEG.	–	–	–	–	–	–	–	–	–	–
INTER.	–	–	–	–	–	–	–	–	–	–
ADV.	8x3	12x3	8x4	12x4	10x4	8x3	12x3	8x4	12x4	10x4
EXP.	8x4	12x4	8x4	12x4	8x5	8x4	12x4	8x4	12x4	10x5

STRENGTH • Arms

WRIST CURLS
Areas worked: Forearms, front of arms
Muscles used: Brachioradialis, biceps

Breathe normally throughout.

PHASE 1

1 With an underhand grip, dead lift a barbell to your thighs (see p. 76), then sit halfway down a bench with your feet flat on the floor.

2 Keep your back flat, abdominals in and head in line with your spine.

3 Lean forward from the waist and place your forearms, palms up, on the bench so that your wrists are slightly over the edge of the bench.

PHASE 2

4 Keeping your forearms firmly on the bench, slowly flex your wrists and curl the barbell toward your body.

5 Hold briefly then under control lower the barbell back over the edge of the bench.

PERSONAL TRAINER'S TIP

This is a weak area in many people, often neglected because the wrists don't have much muscle belly. Weakness here, however, often hinders growth in other muscles, so it is well worth working this area. Start with light weights. You can also use an overhand grip.

	MEN					WOMEN				
WEEKS	1–2	3–4	5–6	7–8	9–10	1–2	3–4	5–6	7–8	9–10
BEG.	–	–	–	–	–	–	–	–	–	–
INTER.	8x2	12x2	8x3	12x3	10x4	8x2	12x2	8x3	12x3	10x4
ADV.	8x3	12x3	8x4	12x4	10x4	8x3	12x3	8x4	12x4	10x4
EXP.	8x4	12x4	8x4	12x4	8x5	8x4	12x4	8x4	12x4	10x5

HALF UP HALF DOWN BARBELL CURLS

Areas worked: Forearms, front of arms
Muscles used: Brachioradialis, biceps

PHASE 1

1 With your hands shoulder width apart, take an underhand grip on a barbell and dead lift it to the front of your thighs (see p. 76).

2 Stand with your back straight, chest lifted and abdominals in. Tilt your pelvis forward.

3 Place your feet shoulder width apart and bend your knees slightly.

4 Keep your upper arms pinned to your body. Relax your shoulders and keep your wrists straight.

5 Bring your elbows to the front of your body for stability. Breathe in.

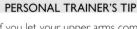

PERSONAL TRAINER'S TIP

If you let your upper arms come away from your body, your back does some of the work, rather than your arms. You can avoid this by standing with your back against a wall for support.

7 Hold briefly, then breathe in as you slowly lower the barbell to your thighs.

8 Complete a set, then return the barbell to waist height.

PHASE 3

9 Pause briefly, then breathe in.

10 Breathe out as you slowly raise the barbell to chest height. Keep your upper arms pinned to your body.

PHASE 2

6 Breathe out as you use your arm muscles to raise the weight to waist height.

11 Hold briefly, then breathe in as you lower the barbell to waist height.

12 Complete a set, then repeat phase 2.

	MEN					WOMEN				
WEEKS	1–2	3–4	5–6	7–8	9–10	1–2	3–4	5–6	7–8	9–10
BEG.	–	–	–	–	–	–	–	–	–	–
INTER.	8x2	12x2	8x3	12x3	10x4	8x2	12x2	8x3	12x3	10x4
ADV.	8x3	12x3	8x4	12x4	10x4	8x3	12x3	8x4	12x4	10x4
EXP.	8x4	12x4	8x4	12x4	8x5	8x4	12x4	8x4	12x4	10x5

133

STRENGTH • Arms

BARBELL CURLS **Areas worked**: Front of arms, forearms
Muscles used: Biceps, brachialis

PHASE 1

1 With your hands shoulder width apart, take an underhand grip on a barbell and dead lift it to the front of your thighs (see p. 76).

2 Stand with your back straight, chest lifted and abdominals in. Tilt your pelvis forward.

3 Place your feet shoulder width apart and turn your toes out slightly. Bend your knees slightly.

4 Tuck your upper arms into your body. Keep your wrists straight and your elbows slightly bent. Breathe in.

PHASE 2

5 Breathe out as you bend your elbows and draw the bar to shoulder height: keep your upper arms pinned to your body.

6 Hold briefly, then breathe in as you lower the bar to your thighs. Keep your elbows slightly bent and wrists straight.

PERSONAL TRAINER'S TIP

To shift the primary emphasis to the brachialis, work reverse curls. Take an overhand grip on the barbell, then follow the directions and repetitions chart for barbell curls.

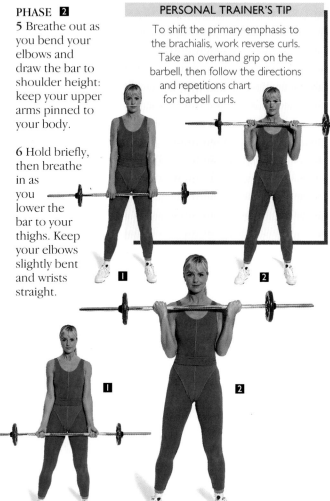

	MEN					WOMEN				
WEEKS	1–2	3–4	5–6	7–8	9–10	1–2	3–4	5–6	7–8	9–10
BEG.	–	–	–	–	–	–	–	–	–	–
INTER.	8x2	12x2	8x3	12x3	10x4	8x2	12x2	8x3	12x3	10x4
ADV.	8x3	12x3	8x4	12x4	10x4	8x3	12x3	8x4	12x4	10x4
EXP.	8x4	12x4	8x4	12x4	8x5	8x4	12x4	8x4	12x4	10x5

TRICEPS KICKBACKS
Areas worked: Back of upper arms
Muscles used: Triceps

PHASE

1 Dead lift a set of dumbbells to your sides (see p. 76), then sit on the end of a bench with your feet flat on the floor, hip width apart.

2 Keeping your back flat and abdominals in, lean forward from the waist. Keep your head in line with your spine.

3 Make sure that your hips and shoulders are square to the front, then raise the weights to the front of your shoulders.

4 Keep your upper arms pinned to your body and your wrists straight. Breathe in.

PHASE 2

5 Breathe out as you slowly press the dumbbells to arm's length behind you. Keep your upper arms pinned to your body and elbows high.

6 Hold briefly, then breathe in as you return the weights to your shoulders.

Note: Keep your abdominals in and remain bent over to take the strain off your neck and back.

WEEKS	MEN					WOMEN				
	1–2	3–4	5–6	7–8	9–10	1–2	3–4	5–6	7–8	9–10
BEG.	–	–	–	–	–	–	–	–	–	–
INTER.	8x2	12x2	8x3	12x3	10x4	8x2	12x2	8x3	12x3	10x4
ADV.	8x3	12x3	8x4	12x4	10x4	8x3	12x3	8x4	12x4	10x4
EXP.	8x4	12x4	8x4	12x4	8x5	8x4	12x4	8x4	12x4	10x5

STRENGTH • Arms

TRICEPS EXTENSIONS   Areas worked: Back of upper arms   Muscles used: Triceps

PHASE 1
1 With your right hand, dead lift a dumbbell to your side (see p. 76), then sit astride a bench with your feet flat on the floor.

2 Keep your back straight, chest lifted and abdominals in. Check that your head is in line with your spine. Place your left hand on your hip.

3 With your wrist straight, raise the weight to your shoulder then under control extend it to arm's length, keeping it in line with your shoulder.

PHASE 2
4 Breathe in as you lower the dumbbell behind your head and down between your shoulder blades.

5 Keep the weight close to your body and your elbow pointing upward.

6 Breathe out as, with a straight wrist, you press the weight back to arm's length.

7 Complete a set with your right arm, then repeat with your left arm.

	MEN					WOMEN				
WEEKS	1–2	3–4	5–6	7–8	9–10	1–2	3–4	5–6	7–8	9–10
BEG.	–	–	–	–	–	–	–	–	–	–
INTER.	–	–	–	–	–	–	–	–	–	–
ADV.	8x3	12x3	8x4	12x4	10x4	8x3	12x3	8x4	12x4	10x4
EXP.	8x4	12x4	8x4	12x4	8x5	8x4	12x4	8x4	12x4	10x5

MACHINE TRICEPS PRESSES   **Areas worked:** Back of upper arms   **Muscles used:** Triceps

PHASE 1

1 Check the pin in the stack.

2 Stand close to the cable with your back straight, chest lifted, abdominals in and head in line with your spine.

3 Place your feet hip width apart. Bend your knees slightly.

4 Take an overhand grip on the bar, with your hands 10–15 cm (4–6 in) apart and your thumbs touching.

5 Keep your knuckles facing forward and your wrists straight.

6 Keep your upper arms and elbows pinned to your body. Try to keep the bar horizontal and close to your body. Breathe in.

PHASE 2

7 Breathe out as you slowly press the bar down to arm's length. Try not to lock your elbows.

8 Try to keep the movement under control: don't jerk the bar.

9 Hold briefly, then breathe in as you return the bar to the start position.

1

2

PERSONAL TRAINER'S TIP

It is important with this exercise to keep the pulling movement smooth and to resist the temptation to jerk the bar downward. Keep your wrists straight throughout.

WEEKS	MEN					WOMEN				
	1–2	3–4	5–6	7–8	9–10	1–2	3–4	5–6	7–8	9–10
BEG.	8x1	12x1	8x2	12x2	10x3	8x1	12x1	8x2	12x2	10x3
INTER.	8x2	12x2	8x3	12x3	10x4	8x2	12x2	8x3	12x3	10x4
ADV.	8x3	12x3	8x4	12x4	10x4	8x3	12x3	8x4	12x4	10x4
EXP.	8x4	12x4	8x4	12x4	8x5	8x4	12x4	8x4	12x4	10x5

STRENGTH • Arms

TRICEPS DIPS Areas worked: Back of upper arms Muscles used: Triceps

PHASE ▮

1 Sit on the side of a bench with your hands, facing forward, on either side of your body.

2 Ease yourself off the bench; keep your back straight, chest lifted and abdominals in. Check that your head is in line with your spine.

3 Extend your legs out in front of you. Bend your knees and place your feet flat on the floor, hip width apart.

PHASE ▮2

4 Breathe in as you slowly lower your body in a straight line toward the floor.

5 Dip as low as your overall strength and flexibility allow.

6 Keep your back close to the bench: it should almost touch it throughout.

7 Hold briefly, then breathe out as you use the strength of your arms (not your legs) to press upward to the start position.

Note: You can, if your prefer, use a chair as support for this exercise, but make sure that it is stable before you begin.

▮1

▮2

PERSONAL TRAINER'S TIP

The farther away from you your legs are, the harder the dip. To make the exercise even more difficult, raise your feet off the floor on a block or chair.

	MEN					WOMEN				
WEEKS	1–2	3–4	5–6	7–8	9–10	1–2	3–4	5–6	7–8	9–10
BEG.	8x1	12x1	8x2	12x2	10x3	8x1	12x1	8x2	12x2	10x3
INTER.	8x2	12x2	8x3	12x3	10x4	8x2	12x2	8x3	12x3	10x4
ADV.	8x3	12x3	8x4	12x4	10x4	8x3	12x3	8x4	12x4	10x4
EXP.	8x4	12x4	8x4	12x4	8x5	8x4	12x4	8x4	12x4	10x5

LYING ELBOW EXTENSIONS   Areas worked: Back of upper arms   Muscles used: Triceps

PHASE 1

1 Dead lift a barbell to your thighs (see p. 76), then sit on the end of a bench with the weight in your lap.

2 Lie on the bench, making sure that your lower back is pressed into the bench but don't force it out of its natural S curve.

3 Place your feet so that you can keep your back down: either on the floor, or on weights or on the end of the bench.

4 Pull your abdominals in and keep your head in line with your spine.

5 With your hands less than shoulder width apart and wrists straight, take an overhand grip on the bar.

6 Press the bar to arm's length.

PHASE 2

7 Breathe in as you slowly lower the bar toward your forehead, bending your elbows and leading with your knuckles. Keep your wrists straight.

8 Hold briefly, then breathe out as you slowly return the barbell to arm's length. Keep your elbows vertical.

9 Take special care on the return that your back stays on the bench.

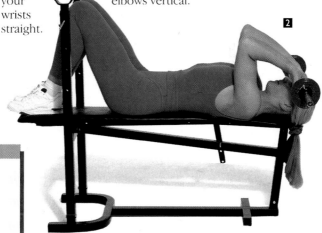

SAFETY TIP

It is especially important to take care when you are lying down and working with weights. Try to have a partner nearby who can take the weight from you if you are having difficulties.

WEEKS	MEN					WOMEN				
	1–2	3–4	5–6	7–8	9–10	1–2	3–4	5–6	7–8	9–10
BEG.	–	–	–	–	–	–	–	–	–	–
INTER.	8x2	12x2	8x3	12x3	10x4	8x2	12x2	8x3	12x3	10x4
ADV.	8x3	12x3	8x4	12x4	10x4	8x3	12x3	8x4	12x4	10x4
EXP.	8x4	12x4	8x4	12x4	8x5	8x4	12x4	8x4	12x4	10x5

STRENGTH • Abdominals

BEGINNERS' CRUNCHES

Areas worked: Abdomen
Muscles used: Rectus abdominis

1 Lie on your back with your knees bent and hip width apart and your feet flat on the floor.

2 Press your lower back firmly into the floor: there should be no arch in your back. Pull your abdominals (abs) in tightly.

3 Keep your head in line with your spine and place both your hands on the front of your thighs. Breathe in.

4 Breathe out as you slowly raise your shoulders off the floor. Don't go too far: this is a small movement. Keep your abs in and your head in line with your spine.

5 As you rise upward, slide your palms up toward your knees. Make sure that your lower back stays down and try to keep the movement smooth.

6 Hold briefly, then breathe in as you slowly lower your shoulders to the floor, without relaxing your abdominals.

7 Brush the floor with your shoulders, then repeat.

WEEKS	MEN					WOMEN				
	1–2	3–4	5–6	7–8	9–10	1–2	3–4	5–6	7–8	9–10
BEG.	8x1	12x1	8x2	12x2	10x3	8x1	12x1	8x2	12x2	10x3
INTER.	8x2	12x2	8x3	12x3	15x3	8x2	12x2	8x3	12x3	15x3
ADV.	12x3	15x3	20x3	25x3	30x3	10x3	12x3	16x3	20x3	25x3
EXP.	30x4	35x4	40x4	45x4	50x4	25x4	30x4	35x4	40x4	45x4

INTERMEDIATE CRUNCHES
Areas worked: Abdomen
Muscles used: Rectus abdominis

PHASE ■
1 Lie on your back with your knees bent and your feet hip width apart and flat on the floor.

2 Press your lower back firmly into the floor: there should be no arch in your back.

3 Pull your abdominals in tightly.

4 Keep your head in line with your spine and cross your hands over your chest. Breathe in.

PHASE ■
5 Breathe out as you slowly raise your shoulders. Don't go too far; this is a small movement. Keep your abs in and your head in line with your spine.

6 Hold briefly, then breathe in as you slowly lower your shoulders to the floor without relaxing your abdominals.

7 Brush the floor with your shoulders, then repeat.

Keep your lower back on the floor

PERSONAL TRAINER'S TIP

This exercise is also suitable at advanced and expert levels. At advanced level, place your hands under your head and follow the directions given in the intermediate exercise. Experts, place one hand behind your head and the other supporting a light weight on your chest. Make sure that your elbows stay back: if they don't, your abdominals are not doing all the work and you risk straining your neck.

STRENGTH • Abdominals

SINGLE ARM CRUNCHES   Areas worked: Abdomen
Muscles used: Rectus abdominis

1 Lie on your back with your knees bent and hip width apart and your feet flat on the floor.

2 Press your lower back firmly into the floor: there should be no arch in your back.

3 Pull your abdominals in tightly and keep your head in line with your spine.

4 Place your right hand behind your head (cupping your head). Place your left hand on the front of your left thigh. Breathe in.

— Aim to touch your knee with your hand

5 Breathe out as you slowly raise your shoulders off the floor. Keep your abs in and head in line with your spine.

6 As you do so, slide your left hand as close to your knee as you can. Keep your lower back down and your right elbow back.

7 Hold briefly, then breathe in as you slowly lower your shoulders to the floor, without relaxing your abdominals.

8 Brush the floor with your shoulders, then repeat.

9 Complete a set then repeat with your left hand cupping your head and your right hand reaching for your right knee.

WEEKS	MEN					WOMEN				
	1–2	3–4	5–6	7–8	9–10	1–2	3–4	5–6	7–8	9–10
BEG.	8x1	12x1	8x2	12x2	10x3	8x1	12x1	8x2	12x2	10x3
INTER.	8x2	12x2	8x3	12x3	15x3	8x2	12x2	8x3	12x3	15x3
ADV.	–	–	–	–	–	–	–	–	–	–
EXP.	–	–	–	–	–	–	–	–	–	–

MACHINE ABDOMINAL CURLS

Areas worked: Abdomen
Muscles used: Rectus abdominis

PHASE 1

1 Check the pin in the stack and the height and depth of the seat (see p. 75).

2 Sit with your back pressed firmly into the back pad and your feet under the foot roller, with your knees hip width apart.

3 Place your hands in the straps provided. Breathe in.

PHASE 2

4 Breathe out as you slowly, and under control, contract your abdominals and curl forward. Don't allow your neck or arms to do the work.

1

2

5 Hold briefly, then breathe in as you slowly return to the start position. Take your time.

SAFETY TIP

If your abdominals are not strong, you may tend to use your back to help with this exercise, which in turn puts it under stress. Don't attempt the exercise unless you are confident that your abdominals are strong.

	MEN					WOMEN				
WEEKS	1–2	3–4	5–6	7–8	9–10	1–2	3–4	5–6	7–8	9–10
BEG.	–	–	–	–	–	–	–	–	–	–
INTER.	–	–	–	–	–	–	–	–	–	–
ADV.	–	–	–	–	–	–	–	–	–	–
EXP.	30x4	35x4	40x4	45x4	50x4	25x4	30x4	35x4	40x4	45x4

STRENGTH • Abdominals

DOUBLE CRUNCHES
Areas worked: Abdomen
Muscles used: Rectus abdominis (upper and lower)

PHASE 1
1 Lie on your back with your legs together and shoulders flat on the floor.

2 Press your lower back firmly into the floor: there should be no arch in your back. Pull your abdominals in tightly.

3 Keep your head in line with your spine.

4 Place your hands behind your head (cupping your head). Keep your elbows pressed back and on the floor.

PHASE 2
5 Breathe out as you bend your knees and raise your shoulders off the floor. Draw your knees and upper body together. Keep your toes pointed away from you and your abs in tightly.

6 Hold briefly, then breathe in as you press your legs away from you and lower your upper body to the floor.

7 Brush the floor with your heels and shoulders, then repeat.

SAFETY TIP
This is a difficult exercise, not recommended for those who have weak abdomens.

	MEN					WOMEN				
WEEKS	1–2	3–4	5–6	7–8	9–10	1–2	3–4	5–6	7–8	9–10
BEG.	–	–	–	–	–	–	–	–	–	–
INTER.	–	–	–	–	–	–	–	–	–	–
ADV.	10x3	15x3	20x3	25x3	30x3	10x3	12x3	16x3	20x3	25x3
EXP.	30x4	35x4	40x4	45x4	50x4	25x4	30x4	35x4	40x4	45x4

LOWER ABDOMEN RAISES

Areas worked: Abdomen
Muscles used: Lower pelvic muscles

PHASE 1

1 Lie on your back with both knees bent and your feet hip width apart and flat on the floor.

2 Press your lower back firmly into the floor: there should be no arch in your back. Pull your abdominals in tightly.

PERSONAL TRAINER'S TIP

For a more advanced exercise, follow the directions for phase 1. Slowly, using your lower abdominals, contract and draw your knees up toward your chest: don't rock. Hold briefly at the top of the movement for maximum effect.

3 Keep your head in line with your spine and place both arms out to your sides. Breathe in.

1

PHASE 2

4 Imagine you have a piece of string attached to your lower abdomen.

5 Breathe out as you slowly pull on the string with your left hand to raise your lower abdomen and lift your hips toward you. Keep your abs contracted.

6 Keep your upper back on the floor.

7 Hold briefly at the top of the movement.

8 Breathe in as you slowly lower your lower back to the floor.

2

WEEKS	MEN					WOMEN				
	1–2	3–4	5–6	7–8	9–10	1–2	3–4	5–6	7–8	9–10
BEG.	8x1	12x1	8x2	12x2	10x3	8x1	12x1	8x2	12x2	10x3
INTER.	8x2	12x2	8x3	12x3	15x3	8x2	12x2	8x3	12x3	15x3
ADV.	12x3	15x3	20x3	25x3	30x3	10x3	12x3	16x3	20x3	25x3
EXP.	30x4	35x4	40x4	45x4	50x4	25x4	30x4	35x4	40x4	45x4

STRENGTH • Abdominals

KNEE RAISED CRUNCHES
Areas worked: Abdomen
Muscles used: Rectus abdominis, lower pelvic muscles

PHASE 1

1 Lie on your back with your knees bent and shoulder width apart and your feet flat on the floor.

2 Press your lower back into the floor: there should be no arch in your back. Pull your abdominals in tightly.

3 Keep your head in line with your spine.

4 Place your hands behind your head (cupping your head).

5 Keeping your foot flexed, raise your right foot so that your toes are level with your knee. Breathe in.

1

PHASE 2

6 Breathe out as you slowly raise your shoulders off the floor. Keep your abs in and your head in line with your spine.

7 As you do so, draw your right knee closer to your chest, keeping your lower back on the floor. Your upper and lower abdominals should form a curve.

8 Hold briefly, then breathe in as you lower your shoulders and return your knee to the start position.

9 Brush the floor with your shoulders, then repeat.

2

		MEN					WOMEN			
WEEKS	1–2	3–4	5–6	7–8	9–10	1–2	3–4	5–6	7–8	9–10
BEG.	–	–	–	–	–	–	–	–	–	–
INTER.	–	–	–	–	–	–	–	–	–	–
ADV.	10x3	15x3	20x3	25x3	30x3	10x3	12x3	16x3	20x3	25x3
EXP.	30x4	35x4	40x4	45x4	50x4	25x4	30x4	35x4	40x4	45x4

TWISTS Areas worked: Abdomen Muscles used: External obliques

PHASE **1**

1 Lie on your back, with your knees bent and hip width apart and your feet flat on the floor.

2 Press your lower back firmly into the floor: there should be no arch in your back. Pull your abdominals in tightly.

3 Keep your head in line with your spine.

4 Place your hands behind your head (cupping your head). Press your elbows back.

5 Cross your right foot over your left knee. Breathe in.

PERSONAL TRAINER'S TIPS

- For an easier exercise, extend your right arm toward your left thigh.
- To extend the exercise, lift your left foot off the floor and rest your ankle on your right thigh, above your knee.

PHASE **2**

6 Breathe out as you slowly, and under control, raise your left shoulder upward and across your body toward your right knee.

7 Twist from the waist, keeping your lower back on the floor and abs in tightly. As you raise your left shoulder, keep your right elbow on the floor.

8 Hold briefly, then breathe in as you slowly lower back down: don't relax your abs.

Keep your neck and shoulders relaxed

9 Complete a set, then repeat raising your right shoulder to your left knee.

	MEN					WOMEN				
WEEKS	1–2	3–4	5–6	7–8	9–10	1–2	3–4	5–6	7–8	9–10
BEG.	8x1	12x1	8x2	12x2	10x3	8x1	12x1	8x2	12x2	10x3
INTER.	8x2	12x2	8x3	12x3	15x3	8x2	12x2	8x3	12x3	15x3
ADV.	12x3	15x3	20x3	25x3	30x3	10x3	12x3	16x3	20x3	25x3
EXP.	30x4	35x4	40x4	45x4	50x4	25x4	30x4	35x4	40x4	45x4

STRENGTH • Abdominals

BICYCLES **Areas worked:** Abdomen
Muscles used: Rectus abdominis, external obliques

1 Lie on your back with your knees bent and hip width apart and your feet flat on the floor.

2 Press your lower back firmly into the floor: there should be no arch in your back. Pull your abdominals in tightly.

3 Keep your head in line with your spine.

4 Place your hands behind your head (cupping your head) and keep your elbows pressed back. Breathe in.

5 Breathe out as you slowly, and under control, draw your left knee toward your chest (keep your abdominals contracted and toes pointed).

6 As you do so, raise your right shoulder to meet your left knee, leading with your elbow.

7 Hold the contraction as high as you can, then breathe in as you slowly lower your shoulder and knee.

8 When you are close to the start position, repeat steps 5, 6 and 7, drawing your right knee and left shoulder toward one another. Don't relax your abs.

9 Try to keep the movement flowing and under control so that your feet and shoulders don't touch the floor.

Keep your abdominals contracted as your arms and legs work

SAFETY TIP

Your abdominals work extremely hard during this exercise, supporting the weight of your torso. Make sure that your lower back stays anchored to the floor and your abs are tight to avoid strain on your back, neck and shoulders.

	MEN					WOMEN				
WEEKS	1–2	3–4	5–6	7–8	9–10	1–2	3–4	5–6	7–8	9–10
BEG.	8x1	12x1	8x2	12x2	10x3	8x1	12x1	8x2	12x2	10x3
INTER.	8x2	12x2	8x3	12x3	15x3	8x2	12x2	8x3	12x3	15x3
ADV.	12x3	15x3	20x3	25x3	30x3	10x3	12x3	16x3	20x3	25x3
EXP.	30x4	35x4	40x4	45x4	50x4	25x4	30x4	35x4	40x4	45x4

MULTICOMBINATIONS Areas worked: Abdomen
Muscles used: Rectus abdominis, external obliques

PHASE

1 Lie on your back with your knees bent and hip width apart and your feet flat on the floor.

2 Press your lower back into the floor: there should be no arch in your back. Pull your abdominals in tightly.

3 Keep your head in line with your spine.

4 Place both hands behind your head (cupping your head) and breathe in.

5 Breathe out as you slowly, and under control, raise your upper body (as in a crunch, p.141).

PHASE **2**

6 Breathing normally, hold, then turn your upper body toward your right knee (as in a twist, p.147).

7 Keeping your abdominals contracted, hold the twist briefly, then, leading with your chest, turn your upper body back to the centre.

PHASE **3**

8 Hold briefly (crunch), then turn your upper body toward your left knee (twist).

9 Hold briefly, then turn your upper body back to the centre.

10 Keeping your abdominals contracted, breathe in as you lower yourself slowly back to the floor.

Note: This is a demanding exercise: keep it under control.

	MEN					WOMEN				
WEEKS	1–2	3–4	5–6	7–8	9–10	1–2	3–4	5–6	7–8	9–10
BEG.	–	–	–	–	–	–	–	–	–	–
INTER.	–	–	–	–	–	–	–	–	–	–
ADV.	–	–	–	–	–	–	–	–	–	–
EXP.	30x4	35x4	40x4	45x4	50x4	25x4	30x4	35x4	40x4	45x4

149

FLEXIBILITY • Introduction

Most people reach the peak of flexibility around the age of ten; after that, over a period of years, the range of movement diminishes as the muscles and tendons around the joints shorten. Those who fare best and whose flexibility remains good are usually those who regularly take some exercise, play sport, do yoga or stretch.

WHY STRETCH?

Stretching helps to lengthen the muscles and tendons, making them more flexible. In the longer term, regular stretching may help to keep you mobile. With age, the joints tend to stiffen: the resulting lack of movement around them causes the tissues that connect them to thicken, reducing their functional range.

The most commonly affected areas are the knees, lower back, hips, fingers and toes. Keeping the tissues around the joints pliable helps to slow down the onset of such common degenerative conditions as osteoporosis and rheumatoid arthritis.

The advantage of a stretching programme over playing a sport more often is that stretching benefits your whole body. You may be able to play a sport despite restricted flexibility in one area, but the chances are that you are compensating for this lack of movement by stressing another area. In the long (or not so long) term, this could be harmful. Your goal should be all-round flexibility, regardless of whether you "need" that flexibility to participate in a certain sport.

HOW TO STRETCH

It is vital to warm up before stretching, either by walking, jogging or skipping, or through a series of exercises such as those described on pp. 36–37.

As you stretch, you should feel mild discomfort. If you hold the stretch, this feeling will slowly diminish. When this happens, you will find it easier to take the stretch a little farther (although you must take care not to force it).

If you feel that the muscle is shaking or wobbling as you try to relax into the stretch, ease off until the feeling has gone. It may be that the muscles were not warm enough; if you have worked particularly hard over the previous few days, they might be unusually tight; or they may just be on the short side. Don't "bounce" to get that bit farther as this puts the muscle under considerable strain.

Concentrate on stretching right into the muscle: if you feel the stretch more in the joint area, then you could be putting stress on the ligaments. Stop and realign your body and start again.

TIMING YOUR STRETCHES

To judge how long to hold a stretch, you need to understand how stretching works. As you stretch a muscle, the "stretch reflex" starts to take effect. This causes the muscle to contract involuntarily (this is the feeling of discomfort as you start to stretch) and prevents you overstretching. After about six seconds, the "inverse stretch reflex", which protects the muscle from excess tension, begins to operate.

To have any effect on your muscle, you have to stretch for longer than six seconds so that the inverse reaction starts. It is a good idea to hold it for 8–10 seconds to be sure. As you become more accustomed to stretching and are more flexible generally, increase the time so that you are holding your stretches for at least 20–30 seconds. This is the point at which muscles start to develop, or lengthen, which is why these longer stretches are usually referred to as "developmental". The fitness menus include both short and long stretches.

Bouncing into a stretch in order to reach further, so-called ballistic stretching, is best avoided. Fast bouncing actions initiate a stretch reflex that causes the muscle to lengthen for 1–2 seconds only; for the rest of the "stretch" it is contracting. Ballistic stretching also causes microscopic tearing of muscle fibres. As a result scar tissue forms which gradually decreases your range of movement around a joint: the opposite of what you are trying to achieve.

DOS AND DON'TS

1 Do stretch every time you exercise, in the warm up before and cool down after the main work of the session.

2 Do check your posture every time. Many people find stretching difficult. Take the time to be sure you have the technique correct.

3 Do try to stretch in the evening when your body is loose. Don't put it off, however, if you can't: stretching in the morning is better than not stretching at all.

4 Don't worry if a partner appears infinitely more flexible than you are. Concentrate on yourself.

5 Do relax: enjoy your stretching.

6 Do make sure you are warm enough. Check the room temperature and have an extra shirt to slip on at the end of the session.

7 Do hold a stretch for 8–10 seconds to maintain muscle length; to increase the length hold the stretch for 20–30 seconds.

FLEXIBILITY • Neck

EASY NECK STRETCH   **Areas worked:** Neck   **Muscles used:** Sternocleidomastoids

Breathe normally throughout.

PHASE ■
1 Stand with your back straight, chest lifted and abdominals in. Tilt your hips forward.

2 Place your feet hip width apart and bend your knees slightly.

3 Relax your shoulders and keep your head in line with your spine.

PHASE ■
4 Slowly drop your left ear toward your left shoulder: don't move your shoulder. Hold the stretch.

5 Repeat, dropping your right ear to your right shoulder.

Note: This stretch, and the one opposite, work equally well if you are sitting down.

PERSONAL TRAINER'S TIP

To extend this stretch, place your left hand on your right ear, and gently press your head toward your left shoulder.

NECK AND SHOULDER STRETCH

Areas worked: Neck, shoulders

Muscles used: Sternocleidomastoids, medial deltoids

Breathe normally throughout.

PHASE 1

1 Stand with your back straight, chest lifted and abdominals in.

2 Place your feet hip width apart and bend your knees slightly.

3 Relax your shoulders, keep your head in line with your spine and put your hands behind your back.

PHASE 2

4 Take your left wrist in your right hand. Lower your right ear toward your right shoulder.

5 Draw your left wrist downward until you can feel the tension in your neck. Hold the stretch.

6 Release your wrist, then your neck. Repeat, left ear to left shoulder.

Note: This is a big stretch for the neck. Take care as you draw your hand down.

WARNING: NECK STRETCHES TO AVOID

X Don't attempt to raise your feet over your head (an exercise often called the plough). This overstretches your neck muscles and could damage your spine.

X Never throw your head right back to stretch the back of your neck. This puts strain on the vertebrae at the top of your spine and can damage the spinal cord.

FLEXIBILITY • Shoulders

OVERHEAD STRETCH   **Areas worked:** Shoulder, back, sides of trunk

Muscles used: Posterior deltoids, latissimus dorsi, obliques

Breathe normally
throughout.

PHASE ▮
1 Stand with your
back straight,
chest lifted and
abdominals in.
Tilt your hips
forward.

2 Place your feet
hip width apart
and bend your
knees slightly.
Keep your head
in line with your
spine.

3 Lifting from
your rib cage,
raise your arms
as far above your
head as you can.

▮

PERSONAL TRAINER'S TIPS

• If you are a
beginner you may
find it easier to
press your palms
together without
crossing your
wrists.
• To extend the
stretch, ease your
arms back slightly.

PHASE ▰
4 Cross your
wrists and place
your palms
together. Keep
your head and
neck up and look
forward. Hold
the stretch.

5 Repeat with
your wrists
crossed in the
opposite way.

▰

SIDE ARM STRETCH Areas worked: Shoulders, back, chest, trunk
Muscles used: Medial deltoids, posterior deltoids, latissimus dorsi, obliques

Breathe normally throughout.

1 Stand with your right side facing, and about 60cm (2ft) away from, a wall.

2 Keep your hips square to the front and your feet hip width apart.

3 Keep your back straight, chest lifted and abdominals in. Make sure that your head is in line with your spine.

4 With your right arm reach up the wall as high as you can and place your palm flat on the wall.

5 Keeping your arm in line with your shoulder, slowly press your armpit toward the wall. Hold the stretch.

6 Turn your left side to the wall, and repeat.

Remember:
Hold a stretch for 8–10 seconds to maintain muscle length; to increase the length hold for 20–30 seconds.

FORWARD ARM STRETCH Areas worked: Shoulders, back
Muscles used: Posterior deltoids, latissimus dorsi

Breathe normally throughout.

1 Stand facing, and about 60cm (2ft) away from, a wall. Keep your back flat, chest lifted and abdominals in.

2 Keeping your head in line with your spine, take a step back with your right foot.

3 Extend your left arm up the wall and place your palm flat on the wall.

4 Reach up with your fingertips and press your armpit close to the wall. Hold the stretch.

5 Repeat using your right arm with your left foot back.

PERSONAL TRAINER'S TIP
To extend this stretch, either reach up with both arms at the same time, or stand farther away from the wall.

FLEXIBILITY • Shoulders

SEATED SHOULDER STRETCH

Areas worked: Shoulders, chest, forearms
Muscles used: Anterior deltoids, pectorals, brachialis

Breathe normally throughout

PHASE ▮
1 Sit with both legs extended out in front of you, with your feet together, and toes pointing upward.

2 Keep your back straight, chest lifted and abdominals in, Make sure that your head is in line with your spine.

3 Put your hands on the floor behind you, with your palms flat on the floor and fingers pointing away from your body. Don't lock your elbows.

PHASE ▮
4 "Walk" your hands behind you as far as is comfortable. Bend your elbows slightly.

5 When you feel tension in your shoulders, hold the stretch.

PERSONAL TRAINER'S TIP
The stretch is easier if you sit with your knees bent and feet hip width apart and flat on the floor.

Keep your back flat and chest lifted

CAT STRETCH   Areas worked: Shoulders, sides

Muscles used: Posterior deltoids, obliques

Breathe normally throughout.

PHASE ◼
1 Kneel in the box position, with your knees hip width apart, back flat, abdominals pulled in and head in line with your spine.

2 Extend your arms out in front of you, with your palms flat on the floor.

> **PERSONAL TRAINER'S TIP**
> You will stretch farther if you avoid pressing your heels to your buttocks: this also puts strain on your knees.

Keep your buttocks high

PHASE ◼◼
3 Slowly press your armpits toward the floor, extending your

hands as far to the front as you can. Keep your head down.

4 When you feel mild tension in your shoulders, hold the stretch.

Note: This stretch is easier if you stand, instead of kneeling, and reach as high as you can with your arms.

FLEXIBILITY·Arms

OVERHEAD TRICEPS STRETCH   **Areas worked**: Back of arms   **Muscles used**: Triceps

PHASE ▮

1 Stand with your back straight, chest lifted and abdominals in. Tilt your hips forward.

2 Place your feet hip width apart and bend your knees slightly. Keep your head in line with your spine.

3 Breathe in as you raise your left arm, bending it at the elbow. Lower your hand between your shoulder blades, keeping it close to your body.

PHASE ▮

4 Throughout this phase, breathe normally. Place your right hand over your left elbow and gently ease your elbow toward the midline of your body.

5 Keep your head up and hold the stretch.

6 Repeat easing your right elbow in your left hand.

> ### PERSONAL TRAINER'S TIP
>
> For an easier stretch place your right hand on the back of your upper arm and press back.

Remember:
Hold a stretch for 8–10 seconds to maintain muscle length; to increase the length hold for 20–30 seconds.

FOREARM STRETCH Areas worked: Forearms Muscles used: Brachialis

Breathe normally throughout.

1 Kneel in the box position (see p. 163), with your back flat, head in line with your spine and abdominals in.

2 Place your palms flat on the floor, with your fingers facing your body and in line with your shoulders.

3 Keeping your palms on the floor, lean back slightly from your hips.

4 When you feel tension in your forearms, pause briefly and hold the stretch.

Note: This is a particularly good stretch for weightlifters.

TRICEPS STRETCH Areas worked: Back of arms, shoulders
Muscles used: Triceps, anterior deltoids

Breathe normally throughout.

1 Stand with your back straight, chest lifted and abdominals in.

2 Relax your shoulders and bend your knees slightly. Tilt your hips forward.

3 Extend your left arm across your chest and place your right hand on the outside of your upper arm.

4 Gently ease your left arm to your chest. Hold the stretch.

5 Repeat, gently easing your right arm with your left hand.

FLEXIBILITY • Back

STANDING BACK STRETCH **Areas worked:** Upper back, shoulders, arms
Muscles used: Trapezius, posterior deltoids, triceps

Breathe normally throughout.

1 Stand with your right side facing, and about 60cm (2ft) away from, a wall.

2 Keep your back straight, chest lifted and abdominals in.

3 Make sure that your hips are square to the front, your feet are hip width apart and your knees are slightly bent. Keep your head in line with your spine.

4 Place your right hand flat on the wall with your fingers pointing forward at, or slightly below, shoulder height.

5 Keeping your hand on the wall, and leading with your shoulder, ease away. Don't lock your elbow. Hold the stretch.

6 Turn your left side to the wall, and repeat.

Remember: Hold a stretch for 8–10 seconds to maintain muscle length; to increase the length hold for 20–30 seconds.

SEATED BACK STRETCH

Areas worked: Back, neck, buttocks

Muscles used: Erector spinae, gluteals, sternocleidomastoids, abductors

Breathe normally throughout.

PHASE ❶

1 Sit with your back straight, chest lifted and abdominals in.

2 Place your hands on the floor at your sides, then bend your right knee and place your right foot flat on the floor on the far side of your left leg.

PHASE ❷

3 Place your left forearm on the outside of your right knee.

4 Place your right hand on the floor behind you, close to your body. Bend your right elbow slightly.

5 Slowly press your right knee toward the midline of your body, then ease your upper body toward your right arm. Twist from the waist.

6 Keeping your head in line with your spine, look over your shoulder.

7 Pause at the point of mild discomfort and hold the stretch.

8 Repeat: cross your left knee over your right leg and turn to the left.

Note: Don't allow your chest and back to collapse as you twist round.

❶

❷

PERSONAL TRAINER'S TIP

This complicated stretch uses several muscle groups. If you are a beginner, you may find it easier to sit cross-legged and twist your head and upper body.

FLEXIBILITY • Back

OPEN BACK STRETCH
Areas worked: Upper back, back of arms
Muscles used: Trapezius, triceps, rhomboids

Breathe normally
throughout.

PHASE 1
1 Stand with your
back straight,
chest lifted and
abdominals in.
Tilt your hips
forward.

2 Place your feet
hip width apart
and bend your
knees slightly.

3 Extend both
arms out in front
of you at chest
height with your
palms together.
Bend your
elbows slightly.

PHASE 2
4 Interlock your
fingers and
reverse your
hands so that
your knuckles
face your body.

5 Slowly extend
both your arms
forward from
your shoulders,
so that your
upper back
opens up.

6 Keeping your
arms at chest
height and
without locking
your elbows,
hold the stretch.

BACK CURL
Areas worked: Entire back **Muscles used:** Erector spinae

Breathe normally
throughout.

1 Lie on your
side. Draw your
knees toward

your chest and
head so that you
are curled into a
tight ball.

2 Make sure that
your head is in
line with your
spine on the
floor.

PERSONAL TRAINER'S TIP
Remember that this is a spine
stretch – for maximum effect bend
your knees and curl up tightly so
that you get a good curve to
your spine.

3 You may find it
useful to put a
towel under
your head for
comfort.

4 Pull your
abdominals in
and relax your
shoulders, neck
and back. Hold
the stretch.

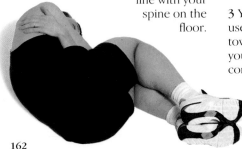

BOX BACK STRETCH   Areas worked: Entire back   Muscles used: Erector spinae

PHASE ▮

1 Kneel in the **box position**: with your knees in line with your hips, hands in line with your shoulders and head in line with your spine.

2 Make sure that your back is flat and pull your abdominals in.

PHASE ▮

3 Breathe in as you slowly hump your back skyward. Keep your abdominals in and tilt your pelvis forward as you lift upward.

4 Pause, breathe normally and hold the stretch.

PHASE ▮

5 Breathe out as you reverse the action, drawing your chest toward the floor. Gently lift your head and push your buttocks up. Don't over-arch your back.

6 Breathing normally, hold the stretch.

FLEXIBILITY • Chest

STANDING CHEST STRETCH Areas worked: Chest **Muscles used:** Pectorals

Breathe normally throughout.

PHASE ❶
1 Stand with your back straight, chest lifted and abdominals in. Tilt your hips forward.

2 Place your feet hip width apart and your hands on your hips. Bend your knees slightly.

3 Keep your head in line with your spine and look forward.

❶

❷

PHASE ❷
4 Squeeze your shoulder blades together, moving your hands round to your buttocks. Keep your head and torso upright and relax your neck and shoulders.

5 When you feel mild tension in your chest, hold the stretch.

Note: This exercise works equally well if you are sitting with your legs extended.

CHEST RAISE Areas worked: Chest **Muscles used:** Pectorals

Breathe normally throughout.

PHASE ❶
1 Lie face down with your hips pressed into the floor and your abdominals pulled in.

2 Check that your head is in line with your spine and tuck your chin down.

3 Interlock your hands and rest them on your buttocks. Bend your elbows slightly.

PHASE ❷
4 Gently ease your shoulder blades together and slowly raise your arms.

5 When you feel mild tension in your chest, hold the stretch.

❶

❷

EASY CHEST STRETCH **Areas worked:** Chest, shoulders **Muscles used:** Pectorals, anterior deltoids

Breathe normally throughout.

1 Stand with your right side facing, and about 60cm (2ft) away from, a wall with your feet hip width apart and knees slightly bent. Tilt your hips forward.

2 Keep your back straight, chest lifted and abdominals in. Keep your head in line with your spine.

3 Place your left hand by your side. Place the palm of your right hand flat on the wall slightly behind you, with your fingers pointing up. Keep this hand at shoulder height.

4 Slowly, leading with your left shoulder, turn away from the wall. Keep your hips square to the front.

5 When you feel tension in your right shoulder, hold the stretch.

6 Turn your left side to the wall and repeat.

Remember: Hold a stretch for 8–10 seconds to maintain muscle length; to increase the length hold for 20–30 seconds.

PERSONAL TRAINER'S TIP
This is also a good shoulder stretch, and can be used in addition to the stretches illustrated on pp. 154–57.

FLEXIBILITY • Buttocks and hips

KNEE HUG   **Areas worked**: Buttocks   **Muscles used**: Gluteus maximus

Breathe normally throughout.

PHASE ▮
1 Lie on your back, place your hands behind your knees and lift your knees toward your chest.

2 Make sure that your lower back is pressed firmly into the floor and pull your abdominals in.

3 Keep your shoulders and neck relaxed and your head in line with your spine throughout.

▮

▮

PERSONAL TRAINER'S TIP

This is an advanced stretch. To make it easier stay in the start position and draw both knees toward your chest.

PHASE ▮
4 Cross your feet at the ankles and place your hands on your lower legs, toward your ankles. Slowly draw your knees toward your chest.

5 When you feel mild tension in your buttocks and outer thighs, hold the stretch.

GLUTEAL STRETCH **Areas worked:** Buttocks **Muscles used:** Gluteals

Breathe normally throughout.

PHASE 1
1 Lie on your back, with both knees bent and your feet flat on the floor.

2 Make sure that your lower back is pressed firmly into the floor and that your abdominals are pulled in.

3 Relax your shoulders and neck and keep your head in line with your spine. Cross your right foot over your left knee.

PHASE 2
4 Slowly raise your left foot off the floor, drawing your knees toward your chest.

5 At the point of mild tension, hold the stretch.

PHASE 3
6 To increase the stretch, lock your hands around your left thigh, straighten your left leg and draw it toward your chest.

7 Repeat, using your right leg.

PERSONAL TRAINER'S TIP

This is an advanced stretch. If at first you find it difficult to keep your shoulders on the floor, try looping a towel around your supporting thigh: this will help to extend the reach from your arms.

FLEXIBILITY • Buttocks and hips

EASY GLUTEAL STRETCH Areas worked: Buttocks Muscles used: Gluteus maximus

Breathe normally throughout.

PHASE **1**
1 Lie with your back pressed firmly into the floor and your head in line with your spine.

2 Bend your right knee and place your foot flat on the floor. Pull your abdominals in.

3 Check that your hips are square and extend your right arm out to your side at about shoulder height. Raise your right foot off the floor.

PHASE **2**
4 Place your left hand on your right outer thigh.

5 Slowly press your right knee across your left leg. When you feel tension in your buttocks and hips, hold the stretch.

PHASE **3**
6 Repeat: draw your bent left knee across your extended right leg and toward the floor. Make sure that your lower back stays pressed down into the floor.

Remember:
Hold a stretch for 8–10 seconds to maintain muscle length; to increase the length hold for 20–30 seconds.

PERSONAL TRAINER'S TIPS

• If you are a beginner, you can make this stretch easier by bending both your knees to one side, then stretching the knee farther from the floor across your body toward the floor.
• To stretch your back rather than your buttocks, draw your knee as close to the floor as you comfortably can: try to keep your body long and symmetrical.

EASY LYING GROIN STRETCH Areas worked: Inner thighs Muscles used: Adductors

Breathe normally throughout.

PHASE ▮
1 Lie on your back with your knees bent and feet flat on the floor.

2 Press your lower back into the floor, pull your abdominals in and tilt your pelvis up.

3 Keep your head in line with your spine and relax your neck and shoulders.

4 Relax your arms and place your palms flat on the floor.

PHASE ▮
5 Bring your heels together and drop your knees apart.

6 Keeping your back flat on the floor, place your hands on your inner thighs and press down.

7 When you feel mild tension in your thighs, hold the stretch.

STANDING GROIN STRETCH Areas worked: Inner thighs
Muscles used: Quadriceps, sartorius

Breathe normally throughout.

1 Stand with your back straight and your feet hip width apart.

Keep your body weight over your hips

2 Keeping your right leg straight, take a big step to the side with your left leg.

3 Bend your left knee and turn your toes out at 45°. Keep your knee in line with your toes.

4 Keeping your hips square to the front and your weight centred, slowly press down into your heels.

5 When you feel mild tension in your groin, hold the stretch.

6 Repeat: turn your right foot out and keep your left leg straight.

FLEXIBILITY • Buttocks and hips

HIP FLEXOR STRETCH
Areas worked: Front of thighs, top of thighs
Muscles used: Sartorius, iliopscas, quadriceps

Breathe normally throughout.

PHASE 1
1 Kneel on the floor on all fours with your hands facing forward.

2 Raise your left knee and align it so that your knee is forward of your ankle. Place your foot flat on the floor. Keep your hips square to the front.

3 Keep your back flat, chest lifted and abdominals in. Make sure that your head is in line with your spine.

PHASE 2
4 Slide your right leg back as far as it will comfortably go. Keep your leg in line with your hip, your knee on the floor and your toes outstretched.

5 Press forward and down from your hips: keep your hips tilted forward.

6 Place your left hand on your left thigh as added support. When you feel mild tension, hold the stretch.

7 Repeat with your left leg extended.

SEATED INNER THIGH STRETCH
Areas worked: Inner thighs
Muscles used: Adductors

Breathe normally throughout.

PHASE 1
1 Sit with your back straight, chest lifted and abdominals in.

2 Keep your head in line with your spine and look forward.

3 Draw your soles together, keeping your knees apart.

PHASE 2
4 Place your forearms on your inner calves and gently press your knees toward the floor. Hold the stretch.

Note: This is an easy stretch, well suited to beginners.

GROIN STRETCH Areas worked: Inner thighs, back of thighs, lower back
Muscles used: Adductors, hamstrings, erector spinae

Breathe normally throughout.

PHASE 1
1 Sit on the floor with your back straight, chest lifted, legs apart and abdominals pulled in tightly.

2 Keep your head in line with your spine.

3 Rest your hands on your inner thighs.

Remember:
Hold a stretch for 8–10 seconds to maintain muscle length; to increase the length hold for 20–30 seconds.

PHASE 2
4 Keeping your torso upright, lift from your waist and bend forward from your hips to place your hands flat on the floor in front of you.

5 Reach forward from your lower back. When you feel mild tension in your groin, lower back and back of thighs, hold the stretch.

PERSONAL TRAINER'S TIP
This is a difficult stretch, requiring good hip flexion. Relax your neck and shoulders and keep your knees and toes pointing up.

FLEXIBILITY • Thighs

EASY QUAD STRETCH
Areas worked: Front of thighs **Muscles used:** Quadriceps

Breathe normally throughout.

1 Lie face down with your legs together.

2 Pull your abdominals in tightly and press your hips firmly into the floor.

3 Rest your head on your left forearm. Keep your head in line with your spine and tuck your chin down.

4 Reach behind with your right hand. Bend your right knee and bring your right foot toward your buttocks. Keep your knees together.

5 Put your right hand around your ankle and ease your foot toward your buttocks. When you feel tension in the front of your thigh, hold the stretch.

6 Repeat using your left leg.

Lifting your knee a little way off the floor increases this stretch.

SIDE ON QUAD STRETCH
Areas worked: Front of thigh **Muscles used:** Quadriceps

Breathe normally throughout.

1 Lie on your right side. Pull your abdominals in and keep your back straight.

2 Bend your right elbow and rest your head on your hand.

3 Check that your head, shoulders and hips are aligned. Bend your right knee slightly for support. Keep your knees and feet together.

4 Slowly bend your left leg and ease your heel toward your buttocks. Place your left hand around your ankle to draw your foot closer.

5 When you feel mild tension in your thigh, hold the stretch.

6 Repeat using your right leg.

Remember:
Hold a stretch for 8–10 seconds to maintain muscle length; to increase the length hold for 20–30 seconds.

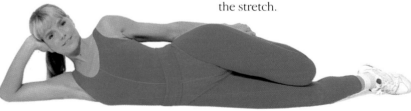

STANDING QUAD STRETCH **Areas worked:** Front of thighs **Muscles used:** Quadriceps

Breathe normally throughout.

1 Stand with your back straight, chest lifted and abdominals in.

2 Place your feet hip width apart and your left hand on the back of a chair for support. Keep your head in line with your spine.

3 Bend your left knee slightly and raise your right leg.

4 Take your right ankle in your right hand and gently ease your foot toward your buttocks. Keep your knees parallel to each other.

5 When you feel mild tension in the front of your thigh, hold the stretch.

6 Repeat, using your left leg.

PERSONAL TRAINER'S TIPS
• You can also use a wall as support for this stretch.
• To increase the stretch, tighten your abdominals and tilt your pelvis forward as you ease your foot up.
• The hip flexor stretch on p. 170 also works the thighs.

Keep your knees hip width apart

Note: Don't arch your back or jerk your foot during this stretch. Also, don't allow your knees to turn outward: this could put your ligaments under stress.

FLEXIBILITY • Thighs

EASY HAMSTRING STRETCH   Areas worked: Back of thighs   Muscles used: Hamstrings

Breathe normally throughout.

PHASE

1 Stand with your feet hip width apart and your toes facing forward.

2 Keep your chest lifted and pull your abdominals in.

3 Take a step forward with your left leg, keeping your leg straight. Bend your right knee and lean forward from your hips.

Keep your back flat

PHASE

4 Keeping your back flat and buttocks high, slowly, leading with your chest, lower your upper body toward your left thigh.

5 Place your hands on the mid-thigh of your right leg. Hold the stretch.

6 Repeat, lowering your chest toward your right thigh.

174

STANDING HAMSTRING STRETCH Areas worked: Back of thighs Muscles used: Hamstrings

Breathe normally throughout.

PHASE ❶
1 Stand with your back straight and abdominals in.

2 Place your feet more than shoulder width apart and half squat. Turn your toes out at 45°.

3 Keep your knees in line with your toes. Place your hands on the top of your thighs.

Keep your hips square to the front throughout

PHASE ❷
4 Lift from your waist and turn your upper body toward your right leg. Lower your chest toward your right knee.

5 Keeping your back straight, place your hands high on your right thigh for support. Look at your thigh.

PHASE ❸
6 Straighten your right leg and lower your chest toward your right thigh. Hold the stretch.

7 Repeat, lowering your chest toward your left thigh.

SAFETY TIP

If you feel any trembling or shaking at any point during this stretch, ease off, bend your knees slightly and start again.

FLEXIBILITY • Thighs

SEATED HAMSTRING STRETCH   Areas worked: Back of thighs   Muscles used: Hamstrings

Breathe normally throughout.

PHASE 1
1 Sit with your back straight, chest lifted and abdominals in. Keep your head in line with your spine.

2 Extend your right leg flat on the floor. Bend your left knee and place the sole of your left foot against your right thigh near to your knee.

3 Raise your arms above your head.

4 Lift from your waist and turn your upper body toward your right leg.

> **PERSONAL TRAINER'S TIP**
>
> To extend this stretch, sit with both legs wide apart on the floor. Bend your knees slightly and point your toes up. Reach for one foot then the other.

PHASE 2
5 Slowly lift your chest and reach for your right foot.

6 When you feel mild tension in the back of your right thigh, hold the stretch.

7 Repeat: bend your right leg and reach for your left foot.

LYING HAMSTRING STRETCH   Areas worked: Back of thighs   Muscles used: Hamstrings

Breathe normally throughout.

PHASE ▯
1 Lie on your back with your lower back pressed firmly into the floor.

2 Pull your abdominals in tightly and make sure that your head is in line with your spine.

3 Keep your shoulders and neck relaxed.

4 Bend both knees and place your feet flat on the floor, hip width apart.

5 Keeping your buttocks on the floor, lift your left leg toward your chest. Place both hands on the back of your thigh for support.

Remember:
Hold a stretch for 8–10 seconds to maintain muscle length; to increase the length hold for 20–30 seconds.

▯

PERSONAL TRAINER'S TIPS

• To increase your arm leverage, wrap a towel around your ankle and draw your leg toward your chest.
• To increase this stretch, draw your knee closer to your head.

PHASE ▮
6 Straighten your left leg and slowly ease it closer to your chest. Move your hands closer to your knee as you do so.

7 If you wobble, place one hand on your calf and the other on your thigh. With your leg as straight as possible, hold the stretch.

8 Repeat, extending your right leg.

Note: If you turn your toes toward your body, this exercise also stretches your calf muscles.

▮

FLEXIBILITY • Calves

UPPER CALF STRETCH **Areas worked**: Back of lower legs **Muscles used**: Gastrocnemius

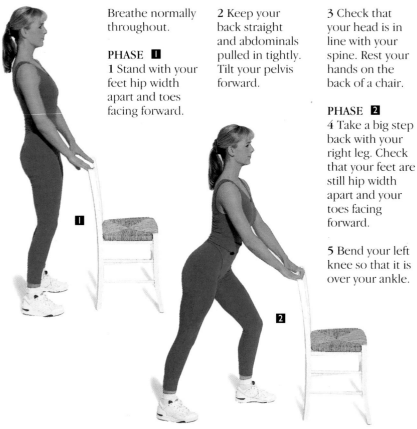

Breathe normally throughout.

PHASE ∎
1 Stand with your feet hip width apart and toes facing forward.

2 Keep your back straight and abdominals pulled in tightly. Tilt your pelvis forward.

3 Check that your head is in line with your spine. Rest your hands on the back of a chair.

PHASE ▨
4 Take a big step back with your right leg. Check that your feet are still hip width apart and your toes facing forward.

5 Bend your left knee so that it is over your ankle.

WARNING: A LEG STRETCH TO AVOID

X Don't attempt to touch your toes with your knees locked. This does not stretch your hamstrings, as is often thought, but it does strain your lower back and causes the vertebrae of your spine to be crushed.

6 Transfer your body weight forward and press your right heel into the floor. Hold the stretch.

7 Repeat, stepping with your left leg. The bigger the step, the greater the stretch.

LOWER CALF STRETCH Areas worked: Back of lower legs Muscles used: Soleus, gastrocnemius

Breathe normally throughout.

PHASE ▮
1 Stand with your back straight, chest lifted and abdominals in. Tilt your pelvis forward.

2 Keep your feet hip width apart, and your head in line with your spine.

3 Place your hands on your waist and your right foot parallel to and slightly behind your left.

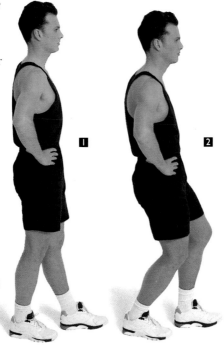

PHASE ▮
4 Keeping your pelvis forward, bend your knees over your toes. Keep your weight toward the front of your toes.

5 When you feel tension in your lower calf, hold the stretch.

6 Repeat with your right foot forward.

Note: Phase 3 of the calf raise on p. 101 is also an effective stretch for the calf muscles.

SEATED LOWER CALF STRETCH Areas worked: Back of lower legs
Muscles used: Soleus, gastrocnemius

Breathe normally throughout.

1 Sit with your back straight, chest lifted and abdominals in. Keep your head in line with your spine.

2 Place your left leg flat on the floor. Point your toes up.

3 Bend your right knee into your chest.

4 Keeping your heel on the floor, take the ball of your right foot in both hands and gently ease it toward your shin. Hold the stretch.

5 Repeat, bending your left knee.

Remember:
Hold a stretch for 8–10 seconds to maintain muscle length; to increase the length hold for 20–30 seconds.

FLEXIBILITY • Abdominals

TOTAL BODY STRETCH

Areas worked: Front of abdomen, sides of trunk, back, legs, arms

Muscles used: Rectus abdominis, obliques, trapezius, quadriceps, triceps

1 Lie on your back with your legs together and extend your arms over your head, in line with your shoulders.

2 Keep your head in line with your spine. Pull your abdominals in tightly and press your lower back firmly into the floor.

3 Take a deep breath in and as you exhale extend both your arms and legs as far away from your body as you can.

4 Breathing normally, hold the stretch.

Note: This exercise works equally well if you stand.

STANDING SIDE STRETCH

Areas worked: Sides of trunk   **Muscles used**: External obliques

1 Take a wide squat position (see p. 84), with your feet turned out and in line with your knees.

2 Keep your back straight and pull your abdominals in. Tilt your hips forward and keep them square to the front.

3 Lift your rib cage and rest your left hand on your left mid-thigh (or side, if that is more comfortable).

4 Make sure that your shoulders are square to the front, and that you are not leaning forward or backward.

5 Breathe in as you extend your right hand over your head.

6 Keeping your rib cage lifted from the waist, lean your upper body to your left. Keep your head in line with your spine.

7 When you feel mild tension in the sides of your trunk and waist, breathe normally and hold the stretch.

8 Repeat, extending your left arm.

180

THE SPHINX   Areas worked: Front of abdomen   Muscles used: Rectus abdominis

PHASE 1
1 Lie face down with your legs together and relaxed, and your hips pressed firmly into the floor.

2 Pull your abdominals in and keep your head in line with your spine.

3 Place your forearms on the floor shoulder width apart. Bend your arms at the elbows and place your palms flat on the floor. Breathe in.

PHASE 2
4 Breathe out as you slowly raise your upper body. Keep your forearms flat on the floor and your hips down.

5 Pull forward and upward from your lower abdomen to your sternum (breast bone) Keep your chin down and neck relaxed.

6 Breathing normally, hold the stretch.

Note: To increase the stretch, extend your arms further forward.

Keep your hips down

SEATED SIDE STRETCH   Areas worked: Sides of trunk   Muscles used: External obliques

PHASE 1
1 Sit with your legs crossed and back straight.

2 Place your right hand on the floor close to your body. Bend your elbow.

3 Extend your left arm above your head.

PHASE 2
4 Keep your buttocks firmly on the floor. Breathe in and, lifting from your waist, reach your left arm over your head.

5 Breathing normally, hold the stretch.

6 Repeat, extending your right arm.

FLEXIBILITY • Assisted stretches

Assisted stretches, as their name suggests, involve working with a partner to improve the degree of a stretch or lengthen its duration. They can be effective in increasing your range of movement around a joint but, because you lose a certain amount of control over your muscles, they must be approached with care.

To derive any benefit at all from this form of stretching, it is vital that you completely trust your partner: if you don't, you will not relax and your muscles won't stretch. It is even more important than usual not to force assisted stretches but to practise them carefully and increase them gradually. If you feel any pain, burning sensation or discomfort, stop.

Finally, a word of warning. If you are going to assist one or more partners on a regular basis, consider taking out personal liability insurance: you can't be too careful.

SHOULDER STRETCH Areas worked: Chest, shoulders Muscles used: Pectorals, anterior deltoids

1 If you are the stretcher, sit on the floor with your back straight and your head in line with your spine.

2 Pull your abdominals in and extend both legs in front of you, with your knees and feet together.

3 If you are the assistant, stand directly behind the stretcher.

4 If you are the stretcher, raise both arms over your head. Keep your chest lifted and back straight.

5 If you are the assistant, press one of your legs into the middle of the stretcher's back to keep the back straight.

6 Gently take hold of the stretcher's arms and slowly extend them up and back. Hold the stretch.

Note: To put less strain on your lower back, sit with your knees bent.

GROIN STRETCH   Areas worked: Inner thighs   Muscles used: Adductors

1 If you are the stretcher, sit with your back straight, your abdominals pulled in and your chest lifted.

2 Relax your shoulders and check that your head is in line with your spine.

3 Keeping the soles of your feet together, relax your knees and drop them apart.

4 If you are the assistant, kneel behind and close to the stretcher and place your hands on his inner thighs.

5 When the stretcher is ready, gently press down on his thighs.

6 At the point of mild tension, hold the stretch.

It is easy to put too much pressure on the thighs – take care

HAMSTRING STRETCH   Areas worked: Back of thighs   Muscles used: Hamstrings

1 If you are the stretcher, lie on your back with your lower back pressed into the floor and your abdominals pulled in tightly.

2 Extend your right leg out in front of you. Raise your left leg, keeping it as straight as you can.

3 If you are the assistant, kneel astride the stretcher's right leg.

4 Take hold of the stretcher's raised left leg (above the knee) and place it over your left shoulder so that your shoulder acts as a brace.

5 Slowly press the stretcher's extended leg toward her chest.

6 At the point of mild tension, hold the stretch.

7 Repeat, raising and stretching the right leg.

Remember: Hold a stretch for 8–10 seconds to maintain muscle length; to increase the length hold for 20–30 seconds.

CIRCUIT TRAINING

Regardless of your degree of motivation, there will probably be times when maintaining your fitness programme can become more of a chore than a pleasure. Circuit training is one way of introducing variety into your programme, which may be all you need to keep it going. It has the added attraction that from warm up to cool down using a circuit can take as little as 45 minutes (the average is about an hour).

Many parks and leisure facilities have circuits but a fixed course is not necessary. The point of a circuit is to set up a number of stations at which you perform a different strength or aerobic exercise. By moving quickly between stations you can increase both your muscular strength and muscular endurance, as well as your aerobic fitness and, to a lesser extent, your flexibility.

GENERAL FITNESS CIRCUITS

If you are putting your own general fitness circuit together, make sure that you have a balance of aerobic and strength stations, and that you work all parts of your body and pairs of muscles: biceps and triceps, quadriceps and hamstrings, and so on.

Use between 4 and 20 different stations, depending on your level of fitness, and don't forget to include a warm up (pp. 36–37) along with short (8–10 second) stretches at the beginning and a

cool down (pp. 38–39) with longer (20–30 second), developmental stretches at the end. It adds interest if you incorporate weights and other pieces of equipment such as a bicycle or rowing machine, but they are not vital. If you do add weights, use only 40–50% of your maximum working weight with a high number of repetitions. This means that you can exercise with good technique for 30 seconds or so and complete 10–15 repetitions comfortably.

Again depending on your level of fitness, you can choose to go from one station to the next with no rest, or incorporate a complete recovery phase in between the stations. You can also include an aerobic activity (gentle at first) in between the "fixed" stations.

There are scores of suitable exercises, including all the strength exercises on pp. 78–149 and the aerobic activities on pp. 58–73. Further aerobic exercises are described on pp. 186–89.

GENERAL FITNESS CIRCUIT		
BEG.	4–6	stations 1–2 circuits
	15–20	seconds on the stations
	20	seconds' rest between stations
INTER.	8–10	stations 2–3 circuits
	20–30	seconds on the stations
	15–20	seconds' gentle activity
ADV.	12–15	stations 3 circuits
	30–40	seconds on the stations
	15–20	seconds' aerobic activity
EXP.	15–20	stations 3–4 circuits
	40–50	seconds on the stations
	10–15	seconds' aerobic activity

The ideal general fitness circuit includes aerobic and muscular strength stations, with alternate exercises for the upper and lower body, to work the whole body.

CIRCUIT TRAINING

MUSCULAR STRENGTH CIRCUITS

Once you have spent a minimum of 10–12 weeks on general fitness circuits, you may want to devise a circuit that works primarily on your muscular strength. When choosing exercises to incorporate, make sure that they will work your whole body. Weights – if you use them – should be heavy enough for you to manage only 8–10 (advanced) or 6–8 (expert) repetitions, with good technique.

It is important to rest between stations for about 30 seconds. If you don't like waiting around to start your next activity, march or jog on the spot. Alternatively, use different body parts at consecutive stations so as not to overstress one particular muscle. In this way, you can reduce your rest time to around 10 seconds.

SPORTS-SPECIFIC CIRCUITS

If you are working with a particular sport in mind (see also pp. 192–97), isolate the muscles you wish to use and include only suitable exercises in the circuit. You may, for example, choose to work only your upper body or your lower body, or your shoulders and so on. If you do work only a specific group of muscles you must rest between stations to avoid overexerting the muscle. If you use weights, work close to your maximum and do a high number of repetitions to enhance both strength and endurance.

MUSCULAR STRENGTH CIRCUIT		
ADV. 12–15	stations	2–3 circuits
30–40	seconds on the stations	
30	seconds' recovery	
EXP. 15–20	stations	3 circuits
40–50	seconds on the stations	
30–40	seconds' recovery	

Among the aerobic exercises that make suitable stations for a circuit are:

SPOTTY DOGS

Breathe normally throughout.

1 Stand with your back straight, chest lifted and abdominals pulled in tightly. Look forward.

2 Keep your legs hip width apart and your feet facing forward.

3 Place your left foot in front of your right. Raise your left arm above your head. Keep your right arm by your side.

4 Jump and change the position of your legs. At the same time lower your left arm and raise your right.

5 Repeat as fast as you can.

JUMPING JACKS
Breathe normally
throughout.

1 Stand with your
back straight,
chest lifted and
abdominals in.
Look forward.

2 Put your feet
flat on the floor
and arms by your
sides. Breathe in.

3 Breathe out as
you jump in the
air, extending
your arms in a
wide arc out to
the sides.

4 Land in a squat
with your toes
turned out at 45°
and your arms
over your head.

5 Make sure that
your knees are in
line with your
feet and don't
extend over
your toes.

6 Press your
heels down as
you land.

7 Breathe in as
you jump back to
the start position.
As you do so,
lower your arms.

8 Repeat as fast
as you can.

> **PERSONAL TRAINER'S TIP**
>
> For an easier exercise that has the
> same effect, place your hands on
> your hips and step to one side.
> Bring your foot back to the centre,
> then step to the other side. Keep
> your hips square, knees in line with
> your toes and feet forward. Don't
> allow your knees to twist outward.

CIRCUIT TRAINING

SQUAT THRUSTS
Breathe normally
throughout.

1 Crouch on the
floor with your
hands more than
shoulder width
apart. Rise up on
to your toes.

2 Pull your
abdominals in,
keep your head
in line with your
spine and look
down.

3 Stick your
buttocks in the
air. Keep your
left leg close to
your chest and
extend your
right leg out
behind you.

4 Change legs.
Don't allow your
back to hollow.

5 Your left leg
should now be
extended behind
you and your
right leg toward
your chest.

6 Repeat as fast
and smoothly as
you can.

Note: Squat
thrusts are only
suitable once you
reach advanced
level.

BURPEES
Breathe normally throughout.

1 Crouch on the floor with your hands more than shoulder width apart in front of you.

2 Pull your abdominals in and keep your head in line with your spine.

3 Jump into the air, extending your arms over your head as you do so. Land with your feet hip width apart.

4 Crouch back into the start position.

5 Jump both legs out behind you, landing on your toes.

6 Jump both legs forward toward your chest.

7 Jump back to the start position and repeat.

Note: This is for experts only.

CROSS TRAINING

The major advantages of cross training – combining different activities to create a comprehensive exercise programme – are that the programme is varied and that it is tailored to your personal needs and goals. And, since all activities work the major muscle groups in slightly different ways, you do not necessarily spend equal time at the sports you choose to combine. Finally, by creating a varied programme, you reduce the risk of repetitive strain injuries.

DEVISING A PROGRAMME

A good way to start putting a cross-training programme together is to make a list of all the activities that you enjoy or would like to try. If you need a partner for some of

them, contact a local gym or club and ask if they know anyone who is looking for a partner. If you can find someone who is at a higher level of fitness than you are, so much the better. Choose activities that, taken together, work all the major muscle groups and all parts of the body. Also, try to ensure that your main activity is the one you enjoy the most.

Whether your programme is intended primarily to build strength or increase aerobic fitness, work on alternate days to give your body time to recover and help your muscles to grow. This also reduces the risk of burn out, fatigue or injury.

Your choice of activities is vast. The table opposite gives just a few of the possibilities. And remember, you don't have to stick to the same programme for ever. Although you are less likely to become bored with a cross-training programme than with other fitness routines, you can still find your enthusiasm waning. If you do, at the end of a 10-week period test yourself again (pp. 22–27) and choose something that you will be able to keep up.

ACTIVITY	Time required for equal aerobic benefit	Strength rating	Aerobic fitness rating
CROSS-COUNTRY SKIING	20 min	medium	high
RUNNING (12km/h:7½mph)	20 min	low	high
JUDO/MARTIAL ARTS	25 min	medium	low
AEROBIC DANCE	30 min	low/medium	high
WATER AEROBICS	30 min	low/medium	high
BADMINTON	30 min	medium	high
SQUASH	30 min	medium	high
VOLLEYBALL	30 min	medium	high
RUNNING (9.5km/h:6mph)	30 min	low	high
ROWING	40 min	medium	medium
STAIR CLIMBING	40 min	medium	medium
SWIMMING	40 min	low	medium
WALKING (8km/h:5mph)	40 min	low	medium
HILL CLIMBING	45 min	medium	medium
CYCLING	45 min	medium	medium/high
TENNIS	45 min	low/medium	medium
BODY CONDITIONING/TONING	60 min	medium	medium
HIKING (rough terrain)	60 min	medium	medium
WEIGHT TRAINING	60 min	high	low/medium

FOR AEROBIC FITNESS
Mon: Step aerobics
Wed: Running
Fri: Cycling
Sun: Power walking

FOR GENERAL FITNESS
Mon: Running
Wed: Circuit training
Fri: Swimming
Sun: Walking

FOR MUSCULAR STRENGTH
Mon: Weight training
Wed: Circuit training
Fri: Weight training
Sun: Martial arts

FOR MUSCULAR ENDURANCE
Mon: Rowing
Wed: Body toning
Fri: Circuit training
Sun: Hill climbing

SPECIALITY MENU • Skiing

If the overriding aim of your fitness programme is to make you more proficient at a particular sport, it is possible to devise a menu that gives priority to specific areas of your body and groups of muscles. Whether you follow one of the suggested menus here, or put together your own for a different sport, work within your fitness level, using the repetitions given in the charts that accompany the strength exercises and the guidelines on circuit training given on pp. 184–89. Use light weights so that you complete the repetitions with good technique.

To improve your skiing ability, both for downhill and cross-country skiing, your speciality menu should include exercises to develop the strength in your legs. The knees in particular come under a great deal of stress in this demanding sport. In order to ski well, you also need good flexibility, especially in your hips and legs, so concentrate on these areas.

Twists, p. 147

SKIING MENU

For lower body strength

Step ups (as step test, p. 23)
Lunges, pp. 78–79
Squats, pp. 80–83
Plié squats, pp. 84–85
Bottom raises, pp. 98–99
Calf raises, pp. 100–101

For upper body strength

Upright rows, p. 110
Lower back raises, pp. 114–15
Lat pull downs, p. 117
Seated rows, p. 119
Bench presses pp. 124–25
Barbell curls, p. 134
Triceps extensions, p. 136

For a skiing circuit

Wall sits, p. 25
Knee lift turn outs, p. 38
Lunges, pp. 78–79
Squats, pp. 80–83
Press ups, pp. 102–4
Triceps dips, p. 138
Crunches, pp. 140–41
Twists, p. 147
Bicycles, p. 148
Single leg squat thrusts, p. 188
Skipping on the spot
Hexagon jumps (jump from a central
point out to the six points of an
imaginary hexagon and back)

Between stations

Choose aerobic activities, such as
jogging or stepping, or the activities
described on pp. 186–89

For flexibility

Stretch your whole body, with
particular emphasis on your legs
(pp. 172–79) and hips (pp. 166–71)

SPECIALITY MENU • Windsurfing

Windsurfing is a demanding activity, requiring good upper body strength, strong legs and good balance. Without these you will find it difficult to pull the boom toward you effectively (and especially difficult to haul it out of the water). The muscles that take the greatest load in windsurfing are the latissimus dorsi, which is the largest muscle in the back, and the erector spinae, the lower back muscle. Good upper-body mobility is also vital to enable you to move the sail into the wind with ease.

As with all sports-specific menus, work within your fitness level, using the repetitions given in the charts that accompany the strength exercises and follow the guidelines on circuit training on pp. 184–89. Use light weights so that you complete the repetitions and build your muscular endurance.

The clean,
pp. 120–21

194

WINDSURFING MENU

For lower body strength

Squats, pp. 80–83
Leg extensions, pp. 86–88
Hamstring curls, pp. 89–91
Calf raises, pp. 100–101

For upper body strength

Lateral raises, p. 105
Upright rows, p. 110
Forward raises, p. 111
Lower back raises, pp. 114–15
Single arm rows, p. 116
Seated rows, p. 119
The clean, pp. 120–21
Barbell curls, p. 134
Triceps extensions, p. 136
Triceps dips, p. 138

For a windsurfing circuit

Squats, pp. 80–83
Calf raises, pp. 100–101
Press ups, pp. 102–4
Lower back raises, pp. 114–15
Triceps dips, p. 138
Crunches, p. 140–41
Twists, p. 147
Bicycles, p. 148

Between stations

Choose aerobic activities, such as skipping or jogging on the spot, or any of the exercises described on pp. 186–89

For flexibility

Stretch your whole body, with particular emphasis on your shoulders (pp. 154–55), back (pp. 160–63) and arms (pp. 158–59)

SPECIALITY MENU • Tennis

If your fitness programme is primarily intended to make you a more effective tennis player, your speciality menu should include plenty of overhead movements that require pushing or reaching actions. You should also concentrate on building strength in your shoulders and upper back and include stretches to increase the overall range of movement around your shoulder joints.

If you want to put together a speciality menu for a different sport or activity, use the menus and information given on these pages as guides. Start by analysing the most important actions or body parts used in the sport to determine which areas and muscles to concentrate on (ask at the gym for help if you are not sure). Choose strength exercises that work the muscles you have pinpointed and don't forget the importance of good all-round flexibility.

Lunges,
pp. 78–79

TENNIS MENU

For lower body strength

Lunges, pp. 78–79
Squats, pp. 80–82
Leg extensions, pp. 86–87
Hamstring curls, pp. 89–91
Inner thigh raises, pp. 92–94
Outer thigh raises, pp. 95–97
Calf raises, pp. 100–101

For upper body strength

Press behind neck, p. 108
Shoulder presses, p. 107
Bent forward lateral raises, p. 109
Upright rows, p. 110
Forward raises, p. 111
Seated rows, p. 119
Bent arm pullovers, p. 129
Wrist curls, p. 132
Barbell curls, p. 134
Triceps extensions, p. 136

For a tennis circuit

Lunges, pp. 78–79
Squats, pp. 80–83
Press ups, pp. 102–4
Triceps dips, p. 138
Crunches, pp. 140–41
Double crunches, p. 144
Twists, p. 147
Side shuffles (take three or four shuffles
to the left and back, then to the right)
Diagonal and square running (across an
area about the size of a service court)

Between stations

Choose aerobic activities, such as
skipping or jogging on the spot, and the
exercises described on pp. 186–89

For flexibility

Stretch your whole body,
with particular emphasis on your
upper body (pp. 152–65 and
pp. 180–81)

JOINING AND USING A GYM

A good health club or gym can offer a great deal in terms of equipment, facilities, and expert supervision and instruction. In addition, many people find that they need the motivation of a class atmosphere, or of others with similar goals, to keep them going.

Make a list of your fitness goals and of all the activities that might interest you. Then visit all the gyms and clubs that are convenient to your home and work place, talk to the staff and instructors and ask questions. If there is a gym that you think meets your needs, visit at least twice before you make a financial commitment, once at peak time and again at the time you are most likely to want to use it.

SITUATION
For it to become a viable part of your fitness programme, the gym must be convenient either to your home or work place. Proximity is vital if you are going to stick to your fitness routine. The gym is going to be a part of your way of life: it has to be convenient. Check that there is adequate parking.

EQUIPMENT
There are numerous makes of equipment and a wide choice of machines. Ask what each machine does and check that everything you need is available. If your goal is aerobic fitness, make sure that there is a range of cardiovascular machines such as treadmills, steps, rowing machines and bicycles.

If you are interested in aerobics, check that the gym has a wooden sprung floor to ensure minimum impact. Carpet and concrete can lead to lower back and leg injuries.

FACILITIES
If you want to use a swimming pool, have a look at it; some clubs advertise pools that are scarcely

A good gym offers a range of adjustable, well-maintained machines that are in good working order. Check before you join that it has every machine you are likely to want to use, and that there are plenty of them: the last thing you want is to have to hang around waiting for a machine to come free.

bigger than jacuzzis. For fitness swimming, you need a pool at least 25m (27yd) long.

Is there a creche, and is it open at all the times you might need it? Check that the shower rooms are clean and that there are adequate locker facilities. Ask whether towels are available for hire. Are there paper towels to wipe the machines down? Is there a water fountain?

ATMOSPHERE

The general atmosphere of the club is an important factor. Are the staff attentive? Do they smile? Do the other members seem to be enjoying themselves? Do they look like the sort of people you might want to know? If you're interested in classes, ask what the maximum attendance is likely to be. Does it seem too many to you?

Most clubs play music during workouts, and this can be very motivating. Does it upset you? Will the club choice motivate you for more than a couple of weeks? Could you use a personal stereo?

STAFF AND TUITION

On your tour of the gym, take note of the attitude of the staff. Are the instructors talking to each other or are they paying careful attention to club members? How do they respond to questions? Is there adequate supervision?

Ask what qualifications the instructors have. If you haven't heard of a qualification, check it out.

FINANCIAL CONSIDERATIONS

Generally, you get what you pay for but there are ways to reduce the financial outlay. Look out for seasonal and promotional offers: you may get a discount if you join as a family, or as a company. Also ask about off-peak membership. If you can make the time to use the gym off peak, this can offer excellent value for money.

Is the club affiliated to others whose facilities you can use at preferential rates?

SAFETY

Reputable clubs ask members to undergo a medical examination, take a fitness test and attend an induction course during which they are shown how to use the machines and familiarized with safety procedures.

Make a note of the safety equipment: is there oxygen, for example? Check that there is always someone on the premises who is qualified in cardiopulmonary resuscitation, life-saving and general first aid.

OTHER SERVICES

Some clubs offer additional services at extra cost: nutritional counselling; lectures and work-shops on such subjects as stress management; massage and beauty treatments. Make sure that those who offer these services are qualified. Don't be intimidated: remember that it is your body.

COPING WITH INJURIES

As soon as you begin to exert your body in new ways, the chances that you will sustain an injury increase. You can't guarantee against injury, but you can minimize the risks. If you understand how your body works and train it well, you are less likely to be troubled by aches, pains, strains and sprains.

You can, for example, choose sports that are suited to your body type (see pp. 18–19). You can also take into account that, although men and women are equally vulnerable to injury, the nature of those injuries tends to reflect the facts that men have greater upper body strength than women, and that women are generally more flexible. Understanding these characteristics and your own body's strengths and weaknesses is the first step toward staying injury free.

TYPES OF INJURY

Muscle soreness is local tenderness when an area is touched and throughout the range of movement. The area often becomes inflamed and the nerve endings irritated by a build up of lactic acid, the main by-product of muscle fatigue.

Muscle soreness affects both the muscle belly and the areas of attachment or points of insertion and usually occurs 24–48 hours after heavy exercise. It is caused by microscopic tearing in the muscle fibres or connective tissues. As you work through a programme, this feeling should ease.

Muscle strain is more acute than muscle soreness and occurs when there are enough tears in the tissues to cause dysfunction in the range, speed and power of movement. Strains are often localized, while soreness tends to be more generalized, and the pain of a strain is sharp rather than dull.

Strains can take anything from a week to a couple of months to heal. See your doctor or go to a sports injuries clinic.

Acute injury is loss of power or a sudden incapacitating pain. Any pain that prevents you from doing a certain movement for 24–48 hours is an acute injury. See your doctor or go to an injuries clinic if it persists.

Chronic injury is one that persists for days, weeks, or even months, despite treatment and rest. It may also recur at intervals thereafter (largely because the surrounding muscles tend to mask a problem until they can do so no longer).

IF YOU ARE INJURED

The first 24 hours after injury are the most critical since these determine the extent of the injury and how quickly you will recover. Immediately after injury occurs, the affected area will be inflamed – red, hot, painful and swollen.

The intensity of the inflammation varies from injury to injury and in fact is the beginning of the healing process, although the body tends to overreact. Your first, vital

THE MOST COMMON INJURIES

Rotator cuff tendonitis: irritation of the muscles and tendons holding the ball and socket of the shoulder joint.
Causes: overuse of the arm overhead, for example in tennis and other racket sports, baseball etc.
Ways to avoid: strengthen the deltoids, trapezuis, triceps, rhomboids, pectorals.

Hamstring pull: pain in the back of thighs.
Causes: lack of strength and flexibility in the hamstrings; weaker hamstrings than quadriceps, which causes an imbalance.
Ways to avoid: work on the hamstrings and quadriceps equally; improve overall flexibility.

Sore patellar tendon: pain in the knees.
Causes: squatting too low and/or too many repetitions; poor technique in leg extensions; inadequate shoes; poor warm up; lack of tone in the surrounding muscles.
Ways to avoid: strengthen the quadriceps, hamstrings and gastrocnemius.

Sore Achilles tendon: inflammation of the tendon attaching the calf muscle to the heel.
Causes: as shin splints.
Ways to avoid: as shin splints.

Whiplash: partial tearing of the neck ligaments.
Causes: forcing the neck into extreme positions.
Ways to avoid: improve mobility of the shoulders and neck; relax muscles by stretching.

Tennis elbow: radiating pain below the elbow.
Causes: racket being too heavy or too tightly strung, straining the forearms; locking the elbows during the swing.
Ways to avoid: strengthen brachialis, triceps, biceps.

Shin splints: acute pain at the front of the lower leg, often felt as pins and needles; area is sore to the touch.
Causes: inadequate shoes, poor surfaces, insufficient warm up.
Ways to avoid: warm up thoroughly, buy correctly fitting shoes (pp. 34–35) suitable for the work surface.

Heel spurs: pain on the underside and back of the arch when you stand up after a rest.
Cause: inappropriate shoes.
Ways to avoid: stretch; wear cushioned shoes; elevate the heel with a heel cushion or cup.

COPING WITH INJURIES

task is to slow the process of inflammation. The easiest way to do this is to remember the acronym ICER: ice, compression, elevation and rest.

Ice To slow the metabolism of the tissues in the affected area, placing them in a sort of "suspended animation", use cold water or an ice pack. (A pack of frozen vegetables is ideal, but wrap whatever you use in a cloth, otherwise you risk a painful burn.)

This limits the damage caused by lack of oxygen and nutrients reaching the area. Leave the ice pack on for no longer than 15 minutes and reapply every two to three hours over the first day.

Compression The spread of the fluids that accumulate as a result of swelling and bleeding can be limited by compression. The easiest way to compress an injury is to apply an elasticated bandage. This should be comfortable and not too tight otherwise it will restrict the blood flow to the area.

Elevation It is advisable to keep any injured part of your body elevated and well supported so that the fluids produced by bleeding and swelling can drain away. In particular, if you sustain an injury to a leg it is vital to keep your leg raised so that the fluids don't pool at your feet.

Rest You cannot work off an injury (in fact in most cases you'll make it worse by trying). All that happens is that although the pain goes, the tissue damage continues. You should rest for a minimum of 24–48 hours. During that time you must protect the injury from further damage so a splint or support may be necessary.

Many people continue to train when injured, in the belief that if they are wearing a belt or wrap they are protecting the injury. This is generally not a good idea. If you are injured for a long time, then a belt can isolate the injured muscle, enabling you to continue working those around it, but under normal circumstances, rest is the best cure (see also p. 77).

So that you can cope with an emergency, always have an ice pack, plasters and bandages to hand. Finally, if you are injured see a doctor or attend a sports injuries clinic. If you continue to work through an injury the swelling and bleeding will spread and you will be susceptible to more problems.

RECOVERING FROM INJURY

After a period of rest, you will probably still feel discomfort or stiffness in the area; this is quite normal. With gentle exercise your body will form a flexible scar across the injured tissues and make further damage less likely.

It is important to strike a balance between enough gentle exercise to move the area and create strong healthy tissues and not so much that you tear the injured tissues once again. If any pain persists stop all exercise; slight stiffness, on the other hand, will eventually ease away. Do plenty of mobility exercises and stretching on the area.

The healing process generally takes about three weeks, after which your body should be ready for more serious exercise. But do take it easy: there is always tomorrow and you don't want to be plagued by recurrent injury.

AVOIDING INJURY

Seemingly minor aches and pains (other than local stiffness as you increase the intensity of your training) are often the telltale signs of a more serious condition under the surface. Have any suspicious ache seen to before it gets worse. Don't leave it until it's too late.

Remember that taking a week off will not have much effect on your overall fitness level: give yourself a break and analyse your programme of exercises. You may need to consider using an alternative exercise for a particular area. **Adequate rest** is essential between workouts, particularly if you are using weights. Muscles don't actually develop while you are working with weights but in the hours following a workout. This is also the time when the body replenishes its energy levels with glycogen and fat (see pp. 210–11).

The longer the workout and the heavier the weights, the longer it takes for the muscle to recover. As your fitness level improves you'll need less rest between workouts, but never take less than 24 hours, especially when you are working the larger muscle groups.

Chronic fatigue sets in if you continue to train when your body has had enough, and this makes you susceptible to injury. Signs of overtraining include a drop in performance even if you feel that you are working hard; aches and pains in your joints, tendons or muscles; loss of strength; tingling, numbness or burning in your limbs; general tiredness; problems sleeping; and constant coughs, colds and other minor ailments.

Take note of what your body is telling you: prevention is always better than cure.

COMMON CAUSES OF INJURY

- lack of warm up
- insufficient cool down
- lack of stretching before and after exercise
- overtraining
- lack of rest
- incorrect footwear
- inadequate equipment
- working against your body type
- ignoring what your body is trying to tell you
- poor technique, particularly in strength exercises
- inadequate teaching
- too many participants in a class
- disregard for safety rules
- not eating enough or well
- habits: smoking, drinking, drugs

YOUR EATING HABITS

Fitness is not only about what you do but also about what you eat. It is impossible to follow an intense fitness-training programme if you are not eating properly: you will not have the energy to keep going.

If you are finding following an exercise programme difficult, or if you suspect that you are not eating healthily, answer yes or no to the following questions .
• Do you drink fewer than 4 large glasses of water a day?
• Do you eat red meat more than 3 times a week?
• Do you eat when you are bored or depressed, or as a reward?
• Do you add salt, sugar, sauces, relishes and toppings to your food?
• Do you finish your children's leftovers?
• Do you drink alcohol more than 3–5 times a week?
• Do you follow calorie- or food-reduction diets?
• Are you aware of how much fat, protein and carbohydrate you eat (see also pp. 206–9)?
• Do you eat a large meal in the evening, then snack in front of the TV and/or before going to bed?
• Do you regularly drink canned fizzy drinks and/or more than 5 cups of tea or coffee a day?
• Do you eat under 3 meals a day?

If the answer to any of these questions is "yes", you may not be eating healthily. If the answer is "yes" to three or more, you should be gradually trying to change your eating habits.

The first thing to do is banish the word "diet" from your vocabulary (see pp. 212–13). Next, keep a list of everything you eat and drink for a week. You now know what you are eating. Don't try to change your habits overnight, but start with some of the worst: substitute poultry for at least one of your meals of red meat, then another. Then, replace one of your poultry meals with pulses and so on. Likewise, start to use low-fat spread instead of butter, gradually weaning yourself off spreads all together. And reduce the amount of alcohol you drink: better still, cut it out.

Eat regularly and try not to eat your main meal of the day in the evening; try not eat anything after about 8 p.m. if you can. Boosting your intake during the day gives you energy that you can burn off; what you eat at night is stored, too often as fat.

At every meal, include at least one of the following: peas, beans, nuts, apples, pears, raisins (or other dried fruit), sweetcorn, brown rice, tuna, Edam or other low-fat cheese, tomatoes, parsnips, carrots, whole-grain cereal, whole-grain bread, unpeeled potatoes, green vegetables, bananas, baked beans (low-sugar), chicken, tofu.

Snacking, in itself, is not a bad thing (and it's certainly better than feeling weak from lack of food). The problem is that most of us snack on things that do not do

A healthy eating programme is reflected in your appearance: clear skin, shiny hair, and eyes with some sparkle. Fresh fruit is the ideal post-exercise booster, a good source of carbohydrate and water.

us any good: biscuits, chocolate (see p. 206), crisps and so on. If you're on the move or going for a session at the gym, carry at least one of the following in your bag: fresh fruit, dried fruit (raisins, currants, dates, figs, but watch how much and drink plenty of water with it), rice cakes (those with sesame seeds have most flavour), cereal bars (check the sugar and fat content, many are suitable), nuts and seeds (almonds, walnuts, sunflower or pumpkin seeds, mixed with dried fruit for an added boost), wholemeal or granary bread or rolls, or wholemeal pitta bread.

NUTRIENTS

We are what we eat: the raw materials from which our bodies are constructed are provided by the food we eat. Normal wear and tear mean that even when we are fully grown our bodies must be maintained and repaired and the materials that do this come from our food. All of the substances that make up our bodies are replaced over a period of around seven years.

The many processes of living – moving, keeping warm and so on – also require fuel energy which comes from food. Most of the foods that we eat are a mixture of protein, fat, carbohydrate, vitamins, minerals and water, the collective term for which is nutrients. Foods with a similar nutrient content are generally grouped together for convenience.

STARCHY AND FLOURY FOODS

This group includes most of the staple foods in most cultures: flour, rice, cereals, potatoes and yams, and products made from these basic foods such as pasta and tortillas. All these foods are rich in carbohydrates, the raw material that the body burns to provide energy (see also pp. 210–11).

Simple carbohydrates are composed of only one or two glucose molecules and are broken down, digested and absorbed quickly. Simple carbohydrates do not occur in nature: they are the result of refining and processing. Cakes, biscuits, chocolate and soft drinks all contain simple carbohydrates and do no good in health terms.

Complex carbohydrates, on the other hand, should form a larger part of most diets than they do at present. These foods, composed of long chains of molecules which are broken down and absorbed slowly, provide sustained energy levels. Complex carbohydrates are found in rice, flour and cereals.

Starchy and floury foods also provide roughage without which the intestines cannot work effectively. If you are eating enough foods that are rich in complex carbohydrates you should have no need for extra fibre.

FRUIT AND VEGETABLES

These are composed of complex carbohydrates and water and are important sources of fibre and vitamins. Fruit and vegetables also provide vitamins A, C and E which play an important role as antioxidants in our bodies. The process of converting food into energy produces oxygen radicals which damage the body's cells, leaving them vulnerable to disease. The ACE vitamins travel around the body, "mopping" up the destructive oxygen radicals.

MILK AND DAIRY PRODUCTS

Dairy products, including milk, are important sources of calcium and protein. Calcium (a mineral, see below) hardens and strengthens

bones and teeth. Proteins are the major building blocks from which all the body's tissues are made. Muscle, skin, bone, hair and blood all have a basic "scaffolding" made from protein.

A high percentage of the animal fat we eat comes from milk and dairy products. Animal fats are widely regarded as major contributors to heart disease and stroke. Skimmed milk and reduced-fat spreads, low-fat yogurts (check the sugar content, which can be high) and low-fat cheeses contain the same amount of calcium and protein as full-fat products, so they are a more sensible choice in health terms.

Vegetables and fruit – the fresher the better – provide much of the colour and flavour in our diets. Try to eat more of them, since as well as being valuable sources of fibre and carbohydrate, they are ideal complements to pulses, cereals and grains.

MEAT, FISH AND EGGS

These foods provide protein, iron and the B vitamins. Oily fish, such as mackerel and sardines, are also good sources of vitamins A and D. Meat also contains fat. In the developed world about 40% of our food energy comes from fat, a rich source of calories (which is why so many westerners are overweight). Dietary thinking now accepts that

NUTRIENTS

this percentage is far too high and that more of this energy should come from carbohydrates.

Generally, red meats have a higher fat content than white meats, which in turn have a higher fat content than white fish. If you don't want to stop eating meat, choose white meat and poultry but try to reduce your overall meat intake.

Many of the nutrients provided by meat, fish and eggs can be found in plant foods. But if you are vegetarian, it is important to vary your diet since most plant foods are not such concentrated forms of protein as animal foods. The richest sources of plant protein are the pulse vegetables: peas, beans, lentils, chickpeas, aduki beans and soya beans, and nuts. Cereals such as rice flour, bread, rice and wheat also provide protein: 90g (3oz) of bread contain as much protein as an egg.

VITAMINS
These are chemicals that the body needs to process other nutrients, help regulate the nervous system and help form genetic materials, hormones and proteins. The best sources of vitamins are fresh foods; storage, especially in daylight, destroys some of the vitamins. And cooking breaks them down so do not boil vegetables, for example, for too long (steaming them is preferable).

If you eat a well-balanced diet, you have no need of vitamin supplements (see also fruit and vegetables, above).

MINERALS
Your body requires minerals – inorganic substances – for forming bones, teeth and blood cells and for regulating body fluids (see also pp. 214–15). Minerals fall into two basic categories, those that you need in relative quantity (although the amounts are still small) such as calcium, phosphorus and magnesium, and those of which you need merely traces. In both cases, however, if you are eating a healthy diet, you will be getting the minerals you need.

THE FOOD PYRAMID
One of the most effective ways to determine whether you are eating healthily is to think of your diet as a pyramid. The height of the pyramid is divided into four equal sections. The base represents complex carbohydrates: the majority of your diet should be composed of these starchy and floury foods. The next vertical tier contains fruit and vegetables, again a significant proportion of your diet.

The next tier up contains meat, fish, eggs, dairy products, pulses and nuts (think how little of any of these you should eat if you eat them all). The pinnacle represents those foods to use only sparingly: fats and simple carbohydrates.

ESSENTIAL NUTRIENTS		
Nutrient	Best sources	Role
Protein	Poultry, white meats, white fish, pulses, nuts	Tissue building, growth and repair
Carbohydrate	Bread, flour, rice, pasta, fresh fruit and vegetables	Provides energy
Fat	Vegetable and nut oils	Forms part of the cells' structure; assists metabolism
Calcium	Skimmed milk, low-fat cheese, yogurt, green vegetables, hard water	Hardens and strengthens bones and teeth, helps blood clotting
Iron	Liver, cereals, chocolate	Needed in manufacture of haemoglobin, the oxygen-carrying compound in the blood
Sodium	Salt	Fluid balance, assists muscle contraction and nerve reaction
Vitamin A	Liver, oily fish, fruit and vegetables	Antioxidant, protects against heart disease and cancer
Vitamin C	Citrus fruits and juices, tomatoes, potatoes	Antioxidant
Vitamin E	Vegetable oils	Antioxidant
Vitamin D	Oily fish, liver, margarine	Helps absorption of calcium

EATING AND EXERCISE

To keep fit, you do not have to understand all the complex processes that convert food into the energy you need. It is important, however, to remember that all the energy you need derives from what you eat.

The complex molecules of fats, carbohydrates and proteins in the foods and drinks you consume are broken down into their smaller constituent molecules in the digestive system. Any of these that the body can use are absorbed, enter the bloodstream and are distributed around the body. Any excesses of useable substances are stored; anything that the body cannot use is eliminated.

The body's cells ultimately store food energy in the chemical adenosine triphosphate (or ATP). When cells split the high-energy bonds of ATP they can harness the energy released, using it either to keep warm, or (in the case of some specialized cells such as muscle cells) to work mechanically, as in running, walking, cycling or swimming.

Glucose is the basic chemical fuel that the cells use most easily. Most of the glucose the body uses derives from carbohydrates in the diet. If there is not enough carbohydrate in the body, glucose can be produced from fat and then from protein (although this can have dangerous consequences since the body needs protein for repair and maintenance).

When you start to exert a muscle, that muscle first uses its stored energy which is soon exhausted. Then, it converts carbohydrates, using oxygen from the bloodstream. Water and carbon dioxide (CO_2) are the waste products of this process. The more vigorous the exercise, the more energy the body requires.

DIETING AND METABOLISM

Many people embark on exercise programmes with the express purpose of losing weight. This may well happen since exercise, above all aerobic exercise such as the activities described on pp. 56–73, boosts your metabolism – the rate

To meet your energy needs, the body processes the carbohydrates in the food you eat, converting it into glucose. This is released into the blood stream and carried to the muscles. There, it breaks down to provide energy, water (so you sweat) and carbon dioxide (which is carried back to the lungs to be exhaled).

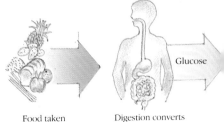

Food taken into body

Digestion converts carbohydrates into glucose

Glucose

at which you convert food into energy and then burn it off.

It is a fact that the metabolic rate decreases with age. Thus, as you get older, you will store food energy, no longer needed by your body to perform its basic functions, as fat unless you increase the amount of exercise you take.

Increasing your metabolism is the only safe and effective way to lose weight. Dieting – in the sense of reducing or radically modifying your food intake overnight – is not a good idea. On a reducing diet, your body's response to the lack of food is to hold on to its reserves for as long as possible. So, as long as you do not cheat with your diet, you do lose weight. Initially this is caused by fluid loss. However, depleting your body's fluid supplies can be harmful.

Your body, still trying to keep its energy reserves intact, then starts to convert muscle tissue into energy, a process that again can be harmful and still does not eliminate the body fat that you want to remove. Finally, your body

can no longer hold on to its reserves and you do start to lose body fat. In order to reach this point, however, you have completely upset the workings of your body, depleted its stores of vitamins and minerals and almost certainly depressed your immune system. This in turn makes you vulnerable to any minor ailment that is prevalent.

Exercise beneficially boosts your metabolism and enables your body to continue to function normally while depleting its reserves of fat. It can also suppress your desire for many of the foods that caused you to be overweight in the first place: alcohol, chocolate and other sweet or fatty "comfort" foods that do no good in health terms.

FAT AND MUSCLE

When you embark on an exercise programme, you should be aware that muscle weighs more than body fat. If you are following a strength-building programme or an all-round fitness programme

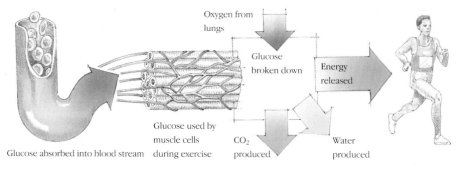

Oxygen from lungs

Glucose broken down

Energy released

Glucose used by muscle cells during exercise

Glucose absorbed into blood stream

CO_2 produced

Water produced

EATING AND EXERCISE

such as those detailed in the fitness menus on pp. 40–55, you may gain weight. This weight will, however, be toned muscle rather than fat. If you weigh yourself regularly (and really there is no need to do so), don't be surprised if this happens. Your changing body shape should be enough to convince you that all is well.

BREAKFASTS

A high complex-carbohydrate start to the day is one of the most effective ways to ensure that you are not reaching for simple-carbohydrate snacks in the middle of the morning. It also helps to boost your metabolism and give you enough energy to want to start the day rather than stay in bed.

The common practice of skipping breakfast, hurrying a sandwich lunch and eating a large meal in the evening can depress your metabolic rate. If you eat late at night, there is no time to use any of the energy produced from the food you consume, so your body stores it (usually as fat). If you want to be a "burner" rather than a "storer", you should follow the old adage: "Breakfast like a king, lunch like a prince, dine like a pauper". This will also ensure that you have the energy to keep going through the day.

Many people claim never to eat breakfast for reasons varying from lack of time to "not feeling like it". This is a tendancy that you should avoid in any case, but once you are on an fitness programme, it is vital to eat breakfast.

You do not have to sit down to several courses: half a banana or a couple of spoonsful of porridge are enough at first. The important point is that you are training your body to want a meal when you get up in the morning. Once you are used to this small amount, start to increase it gradually until breakfast is your main meal of the day.

Be adventurous. Breakfast does not have to be a bowl of corn flakes. In season, choose fresh fruits and freshly squeezed fruit juices, or mix your own cereals from oats, wheat flakes, dried fruit and nuts. The juice of 2 apples, 2 pears and 2 strawberries over a bowl of porridge oats and half a banana tastes wonderful.

CARBOHYDRATE LOADING

Once you start on a fitness programme, you will quickly become fatigued if you do not replenish your energy levels regularly. A snack of a banana, some fresh vegetables, a jacket potato, some dried fruit or rice cakes will give an added boost to your workout.

After a workout, eat a meal high in complex carbohydrates. Keep to unrefined products as far as possible: wholemeal bread and pasta, brown rice and other grains, pulses and nuts, and fresh fruit and vegetables and, again, be adventurous. Most supermarkets today carry ranges of products that ten years ago could only be found in health-food stores. The belief that a high-protein diet was essential for those on fitness programmes, particularly those who wanted to gain muscle, was once widely held. In fact, eating large amounts of protein does not result in muscle gain, since excess is simply stored in the body. It also tends to leave you with little appetite for the carbohydrate foods that you do need.

Some professional sportspeople manipulate their diets and the amount of exercise they take in order to boost the energy stored in their muscles – so-called carbohydrate loading. In this way, they hope to to prolong their capacity for continuous exercise. (Prolonged in these terms means more than 90 minutes.) The belief is that carbohydrate loading is useful if you are running, cycling or swimming over a long distance on a one-off basis. To do this, eat fewer carbohydrates than usual for several days, then in the two to three days before the event, eat far more than usual.

In normal circumstances, carbohydrate loading is not necessary, even when you are fitness training. By eating plenty of carbohydrates (about 60% of your total calorie intake) to meet your increased energy needs you are already boosting your energy reserves to such an extent that carbohydrate loading is redundant.

Fresh fruits and vegetables, whole grains, pulses and pasta are the basis for healthy eating and rich sources of the complex carbohydrates that are essential for anyone following a fitness training programme.

WATER

During exercise, your muscles produce extra heat which must be expelled to keep your body working properly. Sweating is the most obvious way in which this happens. For every 2,400kj (600 calories) of heat energy your body expends, you lose around 1 litre (1¾pt) of sweat. This is increased if you are wearing clothes that don't breathe and allow the sweat to evaporate. Your body remains overheated, producing even more sweat.

You also lose fluid in the form of water vapour in the air you breathe out. The harder and longer you exercise, and the hotter and more humid the environment, the more fluid you lose. During an hour's workout, you can expect to lose 1 litre (1¾pt) of fluid – more if the weather is hot or humid. If you are running or cycling for the same length of time, you can lose twice that amount.

If you carry on exercising without replacing the fluid you have lost, you will become dehydrated. This has adverse effects both on your performance and on your health. When you are dehydrated, it becomes more difficult to exercise and you will tire sooner.

Generally, water comprises 80% of body weight. A loss of just 2% body weight (which is easy if you are sweating hard and not replacing fluid) affects your ability to use your muscles; a 4% loss can cause nausea and vomiting; an 8% loss makes you dizzy and weak, affects your breathing and can make you confused.

Sweat, which is mostly water, also contains small quantities of potassium, sodium and magnesium which must also be replaced. These minerals, collectively known as salts, play an important part in keeping your muscles and nerves functioning properly.

THE REHYDRATION PROCESS

For the fluids you drink to be absorbed into your body, they have to pass from the stomach through the wall of the intestine. If they are less concentrated than the fluids that are already in the intestine (the technical term is "hypotonic"), they will pass through the wall easily and be absorbed quickly.

A dilute glucose solution (less than 4g/2¼ oz glucose per 100ml/ 3½ fl oz water) with some added salts (to replace the lost minerals) is hypotonic. Unsweetened fruit juice diluted with water, with a pinch of sea salt, is the ideal rehydration drink after exercise.

If the fluids you drink are more concentrated than your body's fluids ("hypertonic"), they must be diluted before they can be absorbed. (A drink that is in balance with your body's natural fluids is termed "isotonic" and while it may be a pleasant drink, it will not help to rehydrate you after exercise as well as a hypotonic drink.)

AVOIDING PROBLEMS

As with most things, prevention is better than cure. Don't attempt to exercise unless you are completely hydrated (working out with even a slight hangover is dangerous). If you work out in the morning drink from the time you wake up. Drink plenty before a lunchtime session, and drink all day if you are working out in the evening.

Always take water with you to the gym or an aerobics class, on a run or cycle ride. If you are working at home, have a bottle of water by your side. Drink plenty after a workout.

For normal exercise sessions, water is the best drink before and during. Afterward drink a solution of one part unsweetened fruit juice to three parts water. If the session has been especially hard, or if the weather is hot choose a drink with added electrolytes. After exercise eat carbohydrates: a banana or other fruit, or a rice cake.

SPORTS DRINKS

These are relatively new, designed to tap an increasingly large market. The vast majority are pleasant-tasting and do not do any harm. Likewise, they do little that water, fruit juice and some salt cannot do. Canned fizzy drinks that are not "sports" drinks should be avoided: they offer no benefits at all.

EFFECTS OF DEHYDRATION

If you feel thirsty at any point before or during an exercise session, whatever it is, you are already dehydrated. This will make your workout harder for less achievement, since you will become too tired to work for as long as you would normally choose. The effects of dehydration are:
• increased viscosity of the blood
• less blood pumped to the muscles and skin by the heart
• the need to slow down
• impaired performance and early onset of fatigue
• cramp, which may occur due to loss of fluid rather than loss of salt

SCORECARDS · Planning your programme

The scorecards opposite and on p. 218 are designed for use with the fitness menus; the scorecard on p. 219 complements the endurance programmes.

Choose the scorecard that is most appropriate for you. At beginner and intermediate levels the list of exercises is short, so use the one opposite. Photocopy the page once for each week of your programme, then fill in the exercises, reps and sets that you should be working. Either during or immediately after your workout, fill in the weight you used and note if the actual number of sets and reps you completed was different from that prescribed. Note, too, how you felt:

Were the last couple of reps hard? Could you have done more?

At advanced and expert levels, you may need the scorecard on p. 218 to accommodate the more extensive list of exercises, but the procedure is the same.

If you are concentrating on endurance, photocopy the scorecard on p. 219 once for each week of the programme. Each day record the time and/or distance for your activity. Each programme includes a list of appropriate strength exercises. As you work these fill in the reps, sets and weights columns.

If none of the scorecards meets your precise needs, design your own using these as a guideline.

HOW TO FILL IN YOUR SCORECARD

DAY I	STRENGTH Exercises	Weight	Repetitions & sets
I	Lunges		8x2
2	Box press ups		8x2
3	Inner thigh raises		8x2
4	Lower back raises		8x2
5	Calf raises		8x2
6	Dumbbell curls	3kg (7lb)	8x2
7	Triceps dips		8x2
8	Crunches		8x2
9	Twists		8x2
	ENDURANCE	Time	Distance
Form	Rowing	10 min	n/a
NOTES:	Good workout; felt drained; forgot my water bottle		
DAY 2	STRENGTH Exercises	Weight	Repetitions & Sets
I			
2			
3			

WEEK Nº...... LEVEL................................

DAY 1	STRENGTH Exercises		Weight	Repetitions & Sets
1				
2				
3				
4				
5				
6				
7				
8				
9				
	ENDURANCE		Time	Distance
Form				
NOTES:				

DAY 2	STRENGTH Exercises		Weight	Repetitions & Sets
1				
2				
3				
4				
5				
6				
7				
8				
9				
	ENDURANCE		Time	Distance
Form				
NOTES:				

DAY 3	STRENGTH Exercises		Weight	Repetitions & Sets
1				
2				
3				
4				
5				
6				
7				
8				
9				
	ENDURANCE		Time	Distance
Form				
NOTES:				

WEEK Nº...... LEVEL................................

DAY 1/3	STRENGTH		Repetitions
	Exercises	Weight	& sets
1			
2			
3			
4			
5			
6			
7			
8			
9			
10			
11			
12			
13			
	ENDURANCE	Time	Distance
Form			
NOTES:			

DAY 2/4	STRENGTH		Repetitions
	Exercises	Weight	& sets
1			
2			
3			
4			
5			
6			
7			
8			
9			
10			
11			
12			
13			
	ENDURANCE	Time	Distance
Form			
NOTES:			

WEEK Nº...... LEVEL................................

	ENDURANCE	Time	Distance
Day	Form		
1			
2			
3			
4			
5			
6			
7			

DAY 1	STRENGTH		Repetitions
	Exercises	Weight	& sets
1			
2			
3			
4			
5			
6			

DAY 2	STRENGTH		Repetitions
	Exercises	Weight	& sets
1			
2			
3			
4			
5			
6			

DAY 3	STRENGTH		Repetitions
	Exercises	Weight	& sets
1			
2			
3			
4			
5			
6			

NOTES:

INDEX

Note: Exercises for *flexibility* and *strength* have been indexed under these headings for each body part, after more general information and other exercises. These sections also include exercises that primarily work other areas, but which may be useful.

A

abdomen:
  flexibility 180–1
    the sphinx 181
    total body stretch 180
  strength 140–9
    bicycles 148
    crunches 140–1
      double 144
      knee raised 146
      machine 143
      single arm 142
    lower abdomen raises 145
    multicombinations 149
    twists 147
abdominal hold 25
Achilles tendon, injuries 201
acute injuries 200
advanced menus 48–51
aerobic training:
  circuit training 186–9
  classes 56–7
  cross training 191
  cycling 70–1
  dance 191
  endurance 22, 56–73
  general 10–13
  jogging 60–3
  rowing 68–9
  running 60–3
  shoes 35, 67, 73
  skipping 72–3
  swimming 64–7
  walking 58–9
alarms, personal 31, 63
anaerobic system 12, 13, 68–9, 70
ankles:
  calf raises 100
  weights 31
arms:
  arm swings 36
  injuries 201
  running 63
  side arm reach 36
  walking 58–9

flexibility 158–9
  forearm stretch 159
  open back stretch 162
  overhead triceps stretch 158
  seated shoulder stretch 156
  standing back stretch 160
  total body stretch 180
  triceps stretch 159
strength 130–9
  barbell curls 134
  barbell rows 118
  the clean 120–1
  concentrated curls 131
  dumbbell curls 130
  dumbbell presses 106
  flat bench presses 124
  half up half down barbell curls 133
  incline bench presses 126
  lying elbow extensions 139
  machine exercises:
    bench presses 125
    lat pull downs 117
    seated rows 119
    shoulder presses 107
    triceps presses 137
  press ups 102–4, 122–3
  press behind neck 108
  single arm rows 116
  triceps dips 138
  triceps extensions 136
  triceps kickbacks 135
  upright rows 110
  wrist curls 132
assisted stretches 182–3
ATP (adenosine triphosphate) 12–13, 210, 212

B

back:
  rowing 68
  running 63
  skipping 72
  flexibility 150, 160–3
    back curl 162
    box back stretch 163
    forward arm stretch 155
    groin stretch 171
    open back stretch 162
    overhead stretch 154
    seated back stretch 161
    side arm stretch 155
    standing back stretch 160
    total body stretch 180
  strength 112–21
    back raises 112
    barbell rows 118
    bent arm pullovers 129
    bent forward lateral raises 109
    the clean 120–1
    dead lift 76
    dumbbell presses 106
    lower back raises 68, 70, 114–15
    machine exercises:
      lat pull downs 117
      seated rows 119
      shoulder presses 107
    press behind neck 108
    shoulder shrugs 113
    single arm rows 116
    upright rows 110
backstroke 65, 66, 67
badminton 191
ballistic stretching 151
bandages 202
barbells 30, 31, 74
  barbell curls 67, 134
  barbell rows 68, 118
  the clean 120–1
  dead lift 76
  flat bench presses 124
  half up half down barbell curls 133
  lunges 79
  lying elbow extension 139
  press behind neck 108
  squats 83
  upright rows 110
  wrist curls 132
basketball 73
beginners' menus 40–3

belts 77
bench presses 67, 70
  flat 124
  incline 126
  machine 125
benches 30–1
bent arm pullovers 129
bent forward lateral raises 67, 109
biceps 19
bicycles 70–1
  exercise bicycles 11, 30
  strength exercise 148
blocks 31
body conditioning/toning 191
body types 18–19
bones 14, 15
bottles, water 33
bottom raises 98–9
box back stretch 163
breakfasts 212
breaststroke 66, 67
breathing:
  running 63
  strength training 75
  walking 58
burpees 189
butterfly stroke 66, 67
buttocks:
  dead lift 76
  skipping 72
  flexibility 166–71
    easy gluteal stretch 168
    gluteal stretch 167
    knee hug 166
    seated back stretch 161
  strength:
    bottom raises 98–9
    the clean 120–1
    hamstring curls 89–91
    lunges 78–9
    plié squats 84–5
    squats 80–3

C

calcium 206, 209
calves:
  muscles 19
  running 63
  skipping 72
  flexibility 178–9
    lower calf stretch 179

seated lower calf
    stretch 179
  upper calf stretch 178
  strength:
  calf raises 67, 70, 100–1
  the clean 120–1
  carbohydrate loading
    212–13
carbohydrates 206, 208,
  209, 210, 212, 213
cardiovascular system
  12–13, 56, 64, 70
cartilage 14
cat stretch 157
chairs, comfort 76
chest:
  pains 36
  flexibility 164–5
  chest raise 164
  easy chest stretch 165
  seated shoulder
    stretch 156
  shoulder stretch 182
  side arm stretch 155
  standing chest stretch
    164
  strength 122–9
  bent arm pullovers 129
  flat bench flies 127
  flat bench presses 124
  forward raises 111
  incline bench presses
    126
  incline bench flies 127
  machine exercises:
    bench presses 125
    seated pec decs 128
  press ups 122–3
chronic injuries 200
circuit training 56, 57,
  73, 184–9
classes, aerobics 56–7
the clean 68, 120–1
clothes 32–3
  running 63
  skipping 73
  walking 59
compression, injuries
  202
concentrated curls 131
cooling down 36, 38–9
cramp 69, 215
crawl stroke 65, 66, 67
cross-country skiing
  191, 192

cross trainers 34, 35
cross training 190–1
crunches 70
  beginners' 140
  double 144
  intermediate 141
  knee raised 146
  machine abdominal
    143
  single arm 142
cycling 33, 56, 70–1, 191

D
dairy products 206–7
dance, aerobic 56, 191
dead lift 76
dehydration 63, 214–15
diet 204–11
dizziness 36
double crunches 144
drinking, running 63
dumbbells 30, 31, 74
  bent arm pullovers 129
  bent forward lateral
    raises 109
  concentrated curls 131
  dead lift 76
  dumbbell curls 130
  dumbbell presses 108
  flat bench flies 127
  forward raises 111
  lateral raises 105
  lunges 79
  plié squats 84–5
  shoulder shrugs 113
  single arm rows 116
  squats 82
  triceps extensions 136
  triceps kickbacks 135
  upright rows 110
duration of exercise 29

E
ear plugs 32
easy stretches:
  chest 165
  gluteal 168
  hamstring 174
  lying groin 169
  quad 172
eating 204–13
ectomorphs 18
eggs 207–8
elevation, injuries 202
endomorphs 18

endorphins 60
endurance:
  classes 56–7
  circuit training 186–9
  cross training 191
  cycling 70–1
  jogging 60–3
  muscular 74–5
  rowing 68–9
  running 60–3
  skipping 72–3
  swimming 64–7
  testing 22–3
  training 56–73
  walking 58–9
energy 210–11
equipment 30–1
  clothes 32–3
  shoes 34–5
  swimming 67
exercise bicycles 11, 30
expert menu 52–5.

F
fartlecking 61–2
fat:
  body 18–19, 211–12
  in diet 207–8, 209
fatigue 203
feet:
  running 63
  skipping 72
  walking 59
fibre, dietary 206
fingers, stretching 150
fish 207–8
fitness 10–11
flat bench flies 127
flat bench presses 124
flexibility 10, 150–83
  abdomen 180–1
  arms 158–9
  assisted stretches
    182–3
  back 160–3
  buttocks 166–71
  calves 178–9
  chest 164–5
  hips 166–71
  neck 152–3
  shoulders 154–7
  testing 26–7
  thighs 172–7
food 204–11
forearms *see* arms

forward arm stretch 155
forward flexion 27
forward raises 67, 111
frequency of exercise 29
front crawl 65, 66, 67
fruit 204, 206, 214

G
glucose 210, 214
gluteal stretches 167–8
glycogen 12
goggles 32, 33
grip, dead lift 77
groin stretch 171
  assisted 183
  easy lying 169
  standing 169
gyms 75, 198–9

H
half up half down
  barbell curls 133
hamstrings:
  curls 67, 70, 89–91
  injuries 201
  running 63
  stretches 174–7, 183
hats, swimming 32
heart 12
heart rate:
  measuring 20
  recovery rate 22, 23
  resting 22, 23
  target training zone
    (TTZ) 20, 21
heel spurs 201
helmets, cycling 33
high-impact aerobics 57
hiking 191
hill climbing 191
hips:
  posture 76
  walking 59
  flexibility 166–71
  hip flexor stretch 170
hockey 73
hop scotch 39
hormones 74
hypotonic drinks 214

I
ice packs 202
ICER 202
incline bench presses
  126

incline bench flies 127
inflammation 200–2
injuries 64, 68, 190,
  200–3
inner thigh raises 92–3
intensity of exercise 29
intermediate menus
  44–7
interval training 62, 73
"inverse stretch reflex"
  151
iron 209
isotonic drinks 214

J

jogging 60–3
joints 14, 15
  flexibility testing 26–7
  stretching 150
  warming up 36
judo 191
jumping jacks 187

K

kickboards 67
knees:
  injuries 201
  knee hug 166
  knee lift turnout 38
  knee raised crunches
    146
  skipping 72
  squats 85

L

lactic acid 12, 13, 36,
  69, 70, 200
lat pull downs 67, 68,
  117
lateral raises 105
  bent forward 67, 109
legs:
  cycling 70
  dead lift 76
  injuries 201
  running 60, 63
  skipping 72
  flexibility 172–9
  easy stretches:
    hamstring 174
    lying groin 169
    quad 172
  groin stretch 171
  groin stretch
    (assisted) 183

hamstring stretch
  (assisted) 183
hip flexor stretch 170
lower calf stretch 179
lying stretches:
  groin 169
  hamstring 177
seated stretches:
  hamstring 176
  inner thigh 170
  lower calf 179
  side on quad stretch
    172
standing stretches:
  groin 169
  hamstring 175
  quad 173
total body stretch 180
upper calf stretch 178
strength 78–101
  calf raises 67, 70,
    100–1
  hamstring curls 70,
    89–91
  inner thigh raises 92–4
  leg extensions 67, 70,
    86–8
  lunges 78–9
  outer thigh raises 95–7
  plié squats 84–5
  squats 80–3
lifting 76–7
ligaments 14, 150
low-impact aerobics 57
lower abdomen raises
  145
lower back raises 50, 68,
  70, 114–15
lunges 78–9, 169, 196
lying elbow extensions
  139

M

machine exercises:
  abdominal crunches
    143
  bench presses 125
  hamstring curls 91
  lat pull downs 117
  leg extensions 88
  seated pec decs 128
  seated rows 119
  shoulder presses 107
  triceps presses 137
marathons 61

martial arts 191
meat 207–8
mesomorphs 18
metabolic rate 12–13,
  56, 60, 210–11
milk 206–7
minerals 208, 214
multicombinations 149
muscles 16–17
  anaerobic system 12,
    13
  capacity for
    development 19
  circuit training 186
  cramp 69, 215
  cross training 190, 191
  endurance 10, 74
  energy stores 210–11
  fibres 19
  flexibility testing 26–7
  injuries 200
  strength 10, 24–5,
    74–149
  stretching 150–1
  swimming 67
  weight of 211–12

N

neck:
  injuries 201
  flexibility 152–3
  easy neck stretch 152
  neck and shoulder
    stretch 153
  seated back stretch
    161
nose plugs 32
nutrition 204–11

O

open back stretch 162
osteoporosis 150
outdoor gear 33
outer thigh raises 95–7
overhead stretch 154
overhead triceps
  stretch 158
oxygen 12

P

partners 75, 182
patellar tendon, injuries
  201
PC (phosphate
  creatine) 12

pec decs, machine
  seated 128
pedometers 31, 62
personal stereos 63
plateaus 48
plié squats 84–5
plough 153
plyometrics 57
posture 58, 63, 76, 77
power walking 56, 58–9
press behind neck 108
press ups 24, 102–4,
  122–3
protein 206–8, 209
pulse 20, 31
  see also heart rate
pulses (beans) 208
pyramid, food 208
pyramiding 52

Q

quad stretches 172–3

R

racket sports 73
recovery rate 22, 23
rehydration 214
repetitive strain injuries
  190
reps (repetitions) 75
rest:
  after exercise 203
  circuit training 184, 186
  injuries 202
  running 62
resting heart rate 22, 23
rheumatoid arthritis 150
rotator cuff tendonitis
  201
rowing 56, 68–9, 191
rowing machines 30, 68
rows:
  barbell 118
  machine seated 119
  upright 110
  "runners' high" 60
running 56, 60–3, 191
running shoes 34, 35, 63

S

safety:
  gyms 199
  running 63
  weight training 105
scar tissue 202

scorecards 216–19
seated stretches:
  back 161
  hamstring 176
  inner thigh 170
  lower calf 179
  shoulder 156
  side 181
seated rows 68
sets, strength training 75
shin splints 201
shoes 34–5
  aerobic 67
  and posture 76
  running 34, 35, 63
  skipping 73
  walking 59
shorts 32, 33
shoulders:
  injuries 201
  posture 77
  shoulder extension 27
  shoulder rolls 37
  skipping 72, 73
  flexibility 154–7
  cat stretch 157
  easy chest stretch 165
  forward arm stretch
    155
  neck and shoulder
    stretch 153
  overhead stretch 154
  seated shoulder
    stretch 156
  shoulder stretch 182
  side arm stretch 155
  standing back stretch
    160
  triceps stretch 159
  strength 102–11
  bent forward lateral
    raises 109
  the clean 120–1
  dumbbell presses 106
  flat bench flies 127
  flat bench presses 124
  forward raises 111
  incline bench presses
    126
  lateral raises 105
  machine exercises:
    bench presses 125
    shoulder presses 107
  press behind neck 108
  press ups 102–4, 122–3

shoulder shrugs 113
  upright rows 110
side arm reach 36
side arm stretch 155
side on quad stretch 172
side stretches 180–1
single arm crunches 142
single arm rows 116
sit and reach 26
skeleton 14, 15
ski swings 39
skiing 191, 192–3
skipping 56, 62, 72–3
snacks 204–5
socks 32, 59
sodium 209
speed work 61–2, 66, 71
the sphinx 181
spine, safety 153
  see also back
split routines 54
sports:
  circuit training 186
  speciality menus 192–7
sports drinks 215
spotty dogs 186
sprinting 61–2
squash 191
squat thrusts 188
squats 67, 68, 70, 80–5
stair climbing 191
standing and lifting 76–7
standing stretches:
  back 160
  chest 164
  groin 169
  hamstring 175
  quad 173
  side 180
starchy foods 206
step aerobics 30, 57
step test 23
strain, muscle 200
strength:
  abdominals 140–9
  arms 130–9
  back 112–21
  chest 122–9
  circuit training 186
  cross training 191
  legs 78–101
  sets and reps 75
  shoulders 102–11
  testing 24–5
  training 74–5

"stretch reflex" 151
stretching see flexibility
supersetting 52
supports 77
sweat 63, 214
swimming 56, 64–7, 191
swimming pools 198–9
swimwear 32
synovial joints 14, 15

T
target training zone
  (TTZ) 20, 21
tendonitis 201
tendons 16, 150
tennis 191, 196–7
tennis elbow 201
tennis shoes 35
thighs:
  dead lift 76
  injuries 201
  skipping 72
  flexibility 172–7
  easy stretches:
    hamstring 174
    lying groin 169
    quad 172
  groin stretch 171
  groin stretch
    (assisted) 183
  hamstring stretch
    (assisted) 183
  hip flexor stretch 170
  lying hamstring
    stretch 177
  seated stretches:
    hamstring 176
    inner thigh 170
    side on quad stretch
      172
  standing stretches:
    groin 169
    hamstring 175
    quad 173
  strength:
    the clean 120–1
    hamstring curls 89–91
    inner thigh raises 92–4
    leg extensions 86–8
    lunges 78–9
    outer thigh raises 95–7
    plié squats 84–5
    squats 80–3
  toe clips 33
  toes, stretching 150

total body stretch 180
training shoes 34–5
trampolines 30–1, 62
triceps:
  dips 138
  extensions 136
  kickbacks 135
  presses, machine 137
  stretches 158–9
trunk:
  overhead stretch 154
  seated side stretch 181
  side arm stretch 155
  standing side stretch
    180
  total body stretch 180
twists 147, 193
type of exercise 29

U
up and back reach 37
upright rows 67, 110

V
vegetables 206
vegetarian diet 208
vitamins 206, 208, 209
volleyball 73, 191

W
waist twists 38
walking 56, 58–9, 191
walking shoes 34
wall sits 25
warming up 36–7, 150
water, drinking 214–15
water aerobics 191
weight training:
  belts and supports 77
  circuit training 184,
    186
  cross training 191
  women and 46, 74
  see also strength
weights 31, 40, 42, 44,
  46, 48, 50
whiplash injuries 201
wind resistance 70
windsurfing 194–5
workout benches 30–1
wrists:
  curls 132
  dead lift 77
  skipping 73
  weights 31

ACKNOWLEDGMENTS

The author and publishers gratefully acknowledge the invaluable contribution made by Matthew Ward who took all the photographs in this book, except:
pp. 190–91 C. Pedrotti/Allsport; p. 193 Bob Geldberg/Zefa Picture Library; p. 195 Tom King/The Image Bank; p. 207 Charlie Stebbings; p. 217 Peter Myers.

Illustrators: Chris Forsey pp. 210–11; Annabel Milne pp. 15, 16, 17, 34–35; Coral Mula pp. 10–11, 18–19, 123, 185

The publishers also wish to thank:
Hair and make up: Dawn Lane
Models: Iain Hopkins, Celia Williams
Gym facilities: Latchmere Leisure Centre, London
Wooden props: Simon Haynes
Clothes and shoes worn throughout the exercises:
Woman – Unitard and briefs from The Sanctuary Store
Man – Vest from Nike, shorts from Olympus Sport
All footwear from Nike
Combined set of weights and workout bench used throughout the exercises: Weider Health and Fitness
Other clothes and equipment:
B.M.I. UK/distributor Bolton Stirland International: trampoline pp. 31, 57, 62
Lillywhites: pulse monitor pp. 21, 31; digital stopwatch, pp. 21, 31; Reebok step pp. 23, 30–31; wrist weights p. 31; ankle weights pp. 31, 94, 96, 98–99; pedometer p. 31; skipping rope p. 73
Nike: T-shirt and polo top pp. 190–91
Olympus Sport: Kettler bicycle pp. 11, 21, 30; swimsuit, goggles, earplugs and swimhat pp. 32, 66; tracksuits pp. 33, 59, 62; basketball p. 190; badminton shorts p. 191
On Your Bike: bicycle and cycling accessories pp. 33, 71
Polaris International: webbed gloves p. 32; water dumbbells p. 190
Tuntori UK/distributor Bolton Stirland International: rowing machine pp. 30, 69

AUTHOR'S ACKNOWLEDGMENTS
My thanks go to my best friend and husband Jeremy for supporting me and introducing me to the word processor; Lennie Botter for all her help and advice; Toby for all his encouragement; my clients for being the "case studies" without whom this book would not have been possible; all my friends and family for being there; and Anne Yelland, my editor, for her patience.

I would like to recommend:
Anita Bean's *A Complete Guide to Sports Nutrition* (A & C Black, 1993), which is suitable for anyone on a fitness programme, whatever their level; Steven J. Fleck and William J. Kramer's *Designing Resistance Training Programs* (Human Kinetics Publishers Inc., 1987); and Rex Hazeldine's *Fitness for Sport* (from "The Skills of the Game" series, Crowood Press, 1987).